ADVANCE ACCLAIM

"This is one of those books that every aspiring psychotherapist should be reading. Why? Because it's the clearest, most thorough, most compassionate look inside the work of psychotherapy that I've ever encountered. It's also a book that we seasoned folks might want to consider as a reminder of why we're doing this challenging, rewarding work. This book is like a consult session with one of the best."

—Laura S. Brown, Ph.D., ABPP, Independent Practice of
Consultation and Forensic Psychology, Seattle WA

"A compendium from a highly skilled therapist and accessible author. Books are wrestled into creation, wrought out of lived-experience and wisdom. The word therapist is from the Greek, Θερα′πων—Therapón. In peace-time the Therapón was a King's most-trusted advisor; in war, his personal guard who fought alongside him. This is a brilliant metaphor that fits Robin Shapiro perfectly. *Doing Psychotherapy* will equip and empower you; I will be adding it to my students' required reading."

—Paul Miller, M.D., DMH, MRCPsych, Visiting Professor,
Faculty of Life and Health Sciences, School of Nursing at
Magee Campus, EMDR Europe Accredited Trainer

doing
psychotherapy

A Norton Professional Book

doing
psychotherapy

a trauma and
attachment-informed
approach

robin shapiro

W. W. NORTON & COMPANY

Independent Publishers Since 1923

For information about special discounts for bulk purchases, please contact W. W. Norton
Special Sales at specialsales@wwnorton.com or 800-233-4830

Manufacturing by Sheridan Books
Production manager: Katelyn MacKenzie

ISBN: 978-0-393-71333-6 (pbk.)

W. W. Norton & Company, Inc., 500 Fifth Avenue, New York, N.Y. 10110
www.wwnorton.com

W. W. Norton & Company Ltd., 15 Carlisle Street, London W1D 3BS

1 2 3 4 5 6 7 8 9 0

In loving memory of Tony Ishisaka and Thom Negri, two of my first, and best, teachers.

Contents

Foreword

In this age of manualized treatments, online psychotherapy degrees, and internet addiction, a young therapist might get the impression that doing psychotherapy is like playing a video game. In actuality, psychotherapy in its truest form is a healing relationship, face-to-face, in real time, with a skilled and courageous therapist willing to go with their clients into the dark holes and painful spaces of their inner world. Despite the presence of some gurus selling quick fixes, the search for real teachers and serious professionals gets more difficult every day.

In her brief yet compelling book, Robin Shapiro offers an antidote to the one-size-fits-all notion of psychotherapy. With the presence and warmth of a good teacher who has been there, done that, Robin Shapiro takes a deep dive into the issues at the core of psychotherapy. If you've had the pleasure of being taught or supervised by Robin, you soon realize that her brave, vulnerable, and no-nonsense approach to the human connection is not only educational, but refreshing and often inspiring. Robin's vision of growth, connection, and healing is a perfect match for the way our brains have evolved to connect and grow.

Leveraging her attachment-based perspective and personal style, Robin connects with the reader in a way which provides the model for how to connect with clients. She offers practical strategies as well as frank talk. Modeling an open and supportive stance, her vulnerability successfully invites the reader to be open as well, thus benefiting from her teachings. This approach allows her writing to accomplish something rare in a professional text—the experience of having a teacher sitting next to you as you learn. This book accomplishes this through clear and concise writing, relevant references, and extensive clinical examples.

Throughout, the book addresses general issues of therapy including ethics, boundaries, and diversity as well as specific chapters on the common complaints which bring clients to therapy—anxiety, depression, and addictions. Her chapter on suicide provides the basic facts and a comprehensive list of questions and strategies for dealing with suicidal clients. I certainly wish I had something this useful when I was beginning my training.

In a chapter of central importance, Robin focuses on affect-tolerance. If someone is overly aroused, in other words, if their autonomic nervous system is on high alert, and the brain's ability to learn and problem-solve becomes largely inhibited. The primitive executive, with the amygdala at its core, exerts its veto power over cortical networks of abstract thinking, empathy, and self-awareness. This biological truth is supported by research in epigenetics, biochemistry, and neuroscience - not to mention what every elementary school teacher has learned from experience. By providing a chapter on affect-tolerance and describing practical ways of helping clients regulate themselves, Robin gives readers insight into a fundamental component of any and all successful psychotherapy. And although this book looks at therapy very broadly, Robin's expertise as a trauma therapist is evident.

Whether you are just finishing your clinical training or a seasoned therapist looking for a refresher, the basic principles and practical advice here will help when working with difficult clients after periods of confusion, stagnation, and regression.

Louis Cozolino
Los Angeles, 2019

Acknowledgments

Thank you to everyone who has created healing therapies that give us the many lenses through which to see our clients' problems and the tools to heal them.

Thank you, clients, for everything you are constantly teaching me about how to improve this work.

Thank you, Louis Cozolino, for your excellent Foreword.

Thank you to my two readers, Mark Davila and James Di Donato, who have made this book so much better with their clinical acumen and their quick eyes for grammatical glitches.

Thanks to everyone at Norton, my editor, Deborah Malmud, her assistant, Sara McBride, my copyeditor, Julie HawkOwl, and all the people that make up your wonderful, employee-owned publishing house.

Thank you to Doug Plummer, my beloved husband, for your love, your support, your reading and editing of the book, your great cooking, and for holding down the fort while I wrote yet another book. Thank you for putting up with having me home writing, consulting, and therapizing, when you would rather be making music and not "sneaking around the house."

Thanks to all my supportive friends, in person and online.

This is the first book I've written without the editing assistance of my mother, Elly Welt. I miss our sitting over a printed manuscript and arguing over comma placement. Thank you for teaching me deep reading and for handing down your writing skills. I miss you!

Prologue

Welcome to an amazing profession! This book offers an introductory look at what there is to know about therapy, along with an in-depth explanation of many tools for dealing with the issues and different kinds of people you will encounter in your practice. I will cover how to do a session and a whole therapeutic process; how to connect deeply with every client who walks through your door, and how to use each therapy modality as a lens through which you may see your clients. I want you to know when to get support. I want you to become a lifetime learner of new modalities and to keep honing the ones you have.

I provide clinical consultation to about 50 therapists each month. After 38 years in practice and deep training in many modalities, I run into the same issues in clients, and in consultees, over and over. New therapists often don't know how to start a session or end one. They may not know how to think about gender, or depression, or addiction. While this book can't cover every therapeutic issue in depth, it can give you some clues and a place to start.

When you're done with this book, track down more books, trainings, and conferences whereby you can delve deeply into the material about clients, modalities, and therapeutic issues that interest you. Follow your interests and follow your clients' needs.

In the meantime, know that you are on a steep learning curve. You'll learn in class, in workshops, and from books. However, your clients will be your best teachers. Watch them closely. Listen to everything they say. And continually adjust your modalities and connection to meet each client exactly where they are. Don't see anyone as "the problem." See them as attempted solutions that didn't work out.

And don't forget to enjoy the learning process and the therapy process. The job can be enjoyable. Almost all people who do therapy are lovely, heartful, and serious about healing. What could be better?

doing
psychotherapy

1 / **What Is Therapy?**

Emotionally healthy people are capable of functioning in the world. They are capable of tolerating and regulating their emotions, attaching to loving people, understanding themselves and others, having fun, and finding meaning in their lives.

People who come to therapy are having trouble with some or all of these functions. Psychotherapy is the treatment of clients with emotional and/or behavioral problems; it brings clients to emotional health via interactions with a trained mental health provider.

Psychotherapists use their skills and their connection with clients to promote function, emotional regulation, healthy attachment, understanding, and meaning. Therapists help clients clear the embodied trauma that keeps them braced for danger. They help clients rewire old attachment responses, making new, connectible-but-discerning ones. They help put the clients' functional parts in charge. They assist clients to choose assertiveness over passivity or aggression, to keep a mindful presence in place of dwelling *in* the past or *on* the future, to use/engage skills for negotiating loving relationships and parenting, and how to process the grief when relationships change.

From the first contact to the last session, good therapists are emotionally available, stable, and caring. They accept and respond to all of their clients' emotions, providing reparative experiences for people who lacked, and still lack, adequate responses in their social world. Some therapists challenge thoughts (e.g., cognitive behavioral therapy [CBT]); some focus on emotion (Accelerated Experiential Dynamic Psychotherapy [AEDP]); and some focus primarily on the body (sensorimotor psychotherapy, Somatic Experiencing). Still other therapists work with components of each of these (EMDR, CIMBS). Some therapies focus primarily on the therapeutic relationship as the transformational engine (dynamic therapies, CIMBS). A good therapist, regardless of primary modality, attends to each of these therapeutic components.

"Good therapists are emotionally available, stable, and caring."

Why Do Therapy?

As a therapist, you have the privilege of helping a variety of people heal in the context of deeply intimate relationships, sharing their grief and their triumphs. You get to master new therapies and new situations while taking part in people's transformation. And you get to watch your own affect, tolerance, skills, and understanding grow every day of your practice. In the meantime, you get to make a living and consort with great colleagues who are also dedicated to assisting people in their transformation.

Here are some reasons given by specific therapists' in response to my Facebook post 5/17/2017:

> **Élise S. André:** "What I love about psychotherapy is this: It's real work in association with someone, the 'ahaaaa' moment of integration of a new understanding, transforming the life for the patient. The work itself is a mindful meditative dance like a

pas de deux. It is a gift, the patient is learning, and me too. And I am often amazed with the change occurring in front of me."

Cherie Lindberg: "Sitting soul-to-soul with another human being, holding space, being mindfully present and watching the magic happen."

Shannah Ziatz: "It forces me to be humble, hungry for further knowledge and continued progression, not only for myself or the client, but for the field of science. It makes me want to be better, a better version of myself, that I can emanate to others and make astounding differences in those I serve."

Sabrina Cabassi: "Because with psychotherapy, sometimes miracles happen."

Carrie McMullin: "I love that I get to use both my scientific mind and my creative mind for this work, and that I get constant exposure to what's real in life."

Most psychotherapists love their work. Most love their clients and are loved in return (even if people don't use that language). Therapy is about connecting and healing. This is what attracts people to and keeps people in the profession.

2 / **Therapy Modalities**

What therapies should you use? Short answer: As many as possible. Every therapy is a lens through which to diagnose, explain, and treat a problem. The more lenses through which you can see your clients, the more solutions you have for their problems. If you have only one lens, you may see some clients as untreatable. With many lenses, new solutions may appear. Jerome Frank (1961) offered four components of good psychotherapy:

1. An emotionally charged relationship
2. A therapeutic environment
3. A rationale or myth that provides a plausible explanation for the symptoms
4. A procedure to resolve them

I'd like to add a fifth and sixth component.

5. Give experiences rather than lectures, and
6. Bring in somatic, cognitive, and emotional parts of experience into all interventions.

Somatic therapies, eye movement desensitization and reprocessing (EMDR), ego state therapies, and many others connect with the whole self. When you are learning new therapies, look for which components of awareness they use. And prepare to add whatever the therapy leaves out.

As you assess new clients, look through the lens of several therapies. With each, ask yourself, *"What defines this client's problem? What will this treatment do for this issue? Does this treatment even address this issue? Which treatment or combination will address all of who this client is?"*

At the end of this book, there is a list of Further Resources for each modality.

CBT

Cognitive behavior therapy (CBT) is a widely researched and widely used therapy that involves shifting clients' thinking about their issues, skill-building, and practice shifting attention and mental gears. The CBT lens: How is this thought or feeling dysfunctional, and what do we do to change it? Interventions include thought-stopping and replacing a negative or anxious thought with a better one; and repatterning by clients doing a new more calming or effective behavior, instead of the old dysfunctional one. Nearly all other therapies have some overlap with CBT, especially when discussing disturbing thoughts. CBT is the technique that is taught most in U.S. graduate schools, and is the most researched.

CBT focuses on distorted thoughts as the cause for procrastination, anxiety disorders, trauma responses, poor relationships, and negative feelings. It teaches skills for managing the thoughts and emotions that those thoughts can cause. Although CBT is used for trauma therapy, therapies such as EMDR and somatic therapies can be more effective, since they bring in more components of the body and the brain.

Dialectical behavior therapy (DBT) is

> *"As you assess new clients, look through the lens of several therapies."*

Marsha Linehan's (1993) amalgamation of CBT and mindfulness exercises for emotional regulation. It's especially useful in the treatment of borderline personality disorder and extreme anxiety, and DBT groups are found in many inpatient and outpatient clinics.

EMDR

Eye movement desensitization and reprocessing (EMDR) is also widely researched and validated. The most amazing thing about EMDR is that it makes the effects of trauma go away. It clears simple PTSD in a few sessions. And though it takes longer for EMDR to heal complex trauma, it still deeply impacts clients' internal experience and function. EMDR uses bilateral (back and forth) stimulation via eye movements, sounds, and/or taps on clients while they are attending to their thoughts, emotions, and sensations of dysfunctional memory networks to clear trauma, dissociation, anxiety, addictions, depression, eating disorders, psychosis (Miller, 2016), and a plethora of other symptoms. EMDR's founder, Francine Shapiro (2001), teaches that EMDR sees clients through the lens of the adaptive information processing (AIP) model, which says that trauma, addiction, anxiety, and other disorders are stuck in the brain's neural network, unable to connect with networks that hold adaptive information, and that the bilateral stimulation connects adaptive, present-oriented awareness and emotions to that neural network. In EMDR's three-pronged protocol, clients focus on the first appearance of distress tied to a problem, clear it and other past distress; then they focus on current manifestations; then they focus on how they might deal with future situations. Therapists new to EMDR are amazed at how quickly it can make symptoms disappear. After thirteen years of using CBT and/or hypnotic techniques, I was astonished by EMDR's rapid and total eradication of PTSD symptoms. CBT helped the clients cope with the symptoms. EMDR made them go away. As I learned more and

EMDR—a newer therapy—developed broader applications, I was able to focus the EMDR lens at every presenting problem, including depression, anxiety disorders, relationship issues, chronic pain, immune issues, and addictions.

However, straight EMDR is not enough for many clients. While it makes simple trauma disappear, EMDR is not sufficient for more complex trauma and dissociation. Many practitioners mix ego state interventions with EMDR to prepare clients for trauma processing and/or to assist in the processing of trauma.

Ego State Therapy

For every age and learning situation, we develop neural pathways. We have them for "right now," for every age, and for everything we've learned. When inappropriate old pathways arise (as they do in PTSD or in marital conflict), we need to be able to find "now" and call on our current, safe, strong adult part to run the show. The ego state therapy method gives clients ways to connect the "right now" parts of their brains with the "back then" parts, so that clients can feel and do what's appropriate in the present moment. This therapy fosters understanding of what's happening, for both the client and the therapist. Ego state therapy gets the most functional parts of clients into executive control; it's an excellent therapy for healing trauma; and it's mandatory in work with clients who have personality and dissociative disorders.

Freudian psychoanalysis describes id, ego, and super ego states. Eric Berne took this theory/model further in his transactional analysis therapy, with his Parent, Adult, and Child states. These therapies were about cognitive understanding of the states. Current ego state therapies improve understanding and promote mindful interaction between states, which heals trauma, sorts out dissociative states, and promotes good function.

Hypnotherapy

Hypnotherapy is the ultimate "giving experiences" therapy. Clinical hypnosis creates state changes and often permanent symptom eradication. Hypnotic techniques pervade many other therapies. Hypnotherapists see their modality in guided imagery, ego state work, progressive relaxation, and the sing-song soothing tones used by many therapists. Some consider dissociation, including PTSD, depression, and anxiety as forms of involuntary self-hypnosis. Hypnotherapists "fight fire with fire" by using voluntary inductions to transform symptoms (D. Calof, personal communication, September 3, 2009). Using hypnosis, you can enhance rapport, relaxation, introspection, and awareness of and tolerance for sensations and emotions. You can often shift your client's symptoms first from the front burner to the back burner and then completely out of the kitchen.

Trance Inductions

As you sit in your comfortable chair reading this book, feeling the weight of the book in your hands and the weight of your body in the chair, you may already be wondering if you are in a light trance, and wondering how you know that; noticing how your body might tell you that you know what you know; and you can know that you already know that. You can learn that there are hundreds of trance inductions that I don't have room to teach you, and you can, when you're ready, see some of the many books and resources about them at the end of this book. (That's one induction.)

Inductions are simply ways to help clients focus their attention. They can be as simple as, "Go inside, and find the answer to that question." Or they may involve elaborate ways of showing clients that they're in trance. Formal trance inductions include everything from "you're getting sleepy" to hand levitations and other structured hierarchies of deepening trance. Informal hypnosis may involve constant use of suggestive language ("As you sit on the chair and your eyes close, you might be wondering how deep you can go. And as you notice gravity holding you in that chair and your breath going in and out, you might find that you are going even deeper"), confusion and distraction techniques, storytelling, metaphors, or asking a client to talk to a particular age or part of themself. Good hypnotherapists closely follow their clients' responses, collaborating with both the conscious and unconscious minds. These skills make hypnotherapy a helpful adjunct to any therapy.

Psychodynamic Therapy

Contemporary psychodynamic psychotherapy strives to understand the conscious and unconscious currents that influence a person's mood, thoughts, and behavior patterns. These processes stem from attachment experiences in past and current significant relationships. Through talk and affective experience in the here and now of the therapy moment, psychodynamic therapy attempts to expand the clients' understanding of those experiences to untangle the bind between the relational occurrence and their response to it, so that they can expand their repertoire of responses to the environment—past and present—and can envision a deeper, meaningful life for themselves (H. Arad, personal communication, January 12, 2019). There are hundreds of book and trainings in the classic modes of this therapy.

There are three newer therapy modalities. Habib Davanloo (2000) developed ISTDP (Intensive Short-Term Dynamic Psychotherapy), which is an intense affect-oriented therapy that birthed two other therapies. One of these is Diana Fosha's (2000) AEDP (Accelerated Experiential Dynamic Psychotherapy), which brings in attachment and more support. The other modality, CIMBS (Complex Integration of Multiple Brain Systems) was developed by Beatriz Winstanley Sheldon and Albert Sheldon (in press). CIMBS brings in intense attachment interventions, the body, and a host of brain-and-emotion-shifting techniques. I find

CIMBS, though complicated to learn, the most powerful attachment and mood changer of any that I know.

Somatic Therapies

There are many kinds of movement and somatic therapies. Most share the concept that trauma dysregulates the body, causing restrictions in emotions and movement; that unfinished movements from the time of the trauma need to be experienced and possibly completed; and that attention to sensation and movement will release the trauma, bringing the client's body and brain to a new equilibrium. Most somatic and movement therapies have elements of exposure (remembering the trauma) and mindfulness (noticing present-time experience). Some involve actual movement in the here and now, often completing the held back, repressed, or "undone" action from a traumatic event. Some involve attention to bodily sensations with little or no movement.

From the 1960s through the early 1990s, many movement therapies taught that catharsis was the way to move through old traumas. Clients would punch pillows or the air, kick, sob, scream, and writhe on the floor. After using these therapies, many people, especially those with simple PTSD, found that they had more affect tolerance and more freedom of movement and expression, felt more relaxed and more powerful, and were no longer plagued by PTSD symptoms. Clients with deeper trauma and higher levels of dissociation often remained unhealed or were even damaged by these therapies. For instance, some clients would express their trauma while in a single dissociative state (such as a "fight" emotional part) without integrating their experience, thus having the same experience over and over with temporary state changes but no long-term change of symptoms. Others would decompensate to the point of hospitalization or be triggered to act out old scenarios on unsuspecting staff or members of their movement therapy group.

Newer somatic therapies move more slowly, tracking clients closely as they track their own process. They often include relational or emotional holding by the therapist and have less emphasis on catharsis and more emphasis on rebalancing the nervous system through slow attention to sensation and affect. They are helpful for people who feel stuck; for processing trauma; for learning to feel, accept, and express emotion; and for combining with almost any other therapy.

Somatic therapies include Peter Levine's Somatic Experiencing (SE; Levine, 1997), which helps clients "pendulate" between positive innate orienting responses and the freeze response or an active, defensive bodily state. Clients are coached to stay with the subsequent shaking and release of pent-up energy, then they are directed to notice the next bodily area of tension and holding. Clients might imagine running away or fighting back and note the body's response to their imaginal actions. Therapists continue this process until the tension and trauma reactions dissipate and the client is in a relaxed and energized state of equilibrium. SE is helpful for trauma but lacks the attachment components necessary for working with many complex trauma clients. SE techniques work well in combination with attachment-oriented therapies and in the context of a good, containing therapeutic relationship.

"Learn as many modalities as you can. You owe your clients the best and most suitable interventions for their issues."

Sensorimotor psychotherapy (SP), which was developed by Pat Ogden in the 1980s and continues to evolve, is a "body-oriented talking therapy" that intentionally integrates psychotherapy and body therapy (Ogden, Minton, & Pain, 2006). SP helps clients stabilize, release, and heal the physiological symptoms of trauma, attachment failure, grief and loss, and developmental arrest by using a wide range of somatic interventions, woven seamlessly into the psychotherapeutic process.

Sharon Stanley (2016) teaches somatic transformation, which includes interpersonal neurobiology, attachment throughout the life cycle, healing dissociative disorders, and somatic therapy within a relational model of therapy. She integrates somatic processes with depth psychology and teaches a rich, somatically based, psychotherapy-informed way of working.

Conclusion

Learn as many modalities as you can. You owe your clients the best and most suitable interventions for their issues. And you owe yourself the excitement of new lenses, new methods, constant growth, and the knowledge that you are serving your clients in the best ways possible. Make sure you don't overwhelm yourself with too many trainings at once. When you've nailed one, then you can move onto the next. It makes the work more fun and much more effective.

3 / **How to Start**

You have several tasks in the first session: begin to establish the therapeutic relationship, start your assessment, co-create a plan to meet goals, and set the structure of therapy in terms of frequency, availability, payment, and boundaries, along with other details. Robert Taibbi (2016) says you also want to "sell" the therapy: getting the client to buy-in to the plan. If you have email or telephone contact with the client, your job starts there. You may have already established when you are available and asked them to bring in a list of what differences they want to see in their lives as a result of therapy.

Disclosures

Much of the information about therapy structure will be in your, or your organization's, disclosure statement. Ideally, your client will have read the statement before the first session, and you and the client will sign and date it in the first few minutes, after you've asked if there are any questions. While the exact expectations vary by state and professional license, disclosures contain information about payment, scheduling, confidentiality, and when confidentiality may be broken. They are read and signed at the beginning of the first session. Disclosure statements should include your contact information; your clinical qualifications and modalities; your license number; "the right of clients to refuse treatment; the extent of confidentiality provided by law; billing information, including fees, insurance, etc.; contact information for your local Department of Health contact for the list of possible professional contact; and contact information for your state's health professions complaint process" (Anderson, 2011). You can find your state's mandated disclosure statements through your state's professional association (for social workers, counselors, MFTs, psychologists, etc.).

Beginning

Nearly every new client is anxious about sharing their shortcomings, distress, and vulnerabilities with a stranger. Most clients worry that they are unhealable or that you may not be the right one to help them. From the very first contact, be warm, curious, and clear that you are in a collaborative relationship. Start with some version of "I'm happy to meet you!" Explain what they can expect from the first session, *"Our job today, is to start to know each other; for me to know what you want out of therapy; and to start figuring out how to meet those goals. I'll be asking you a lot of questions so that we will know what we're doing and why."* Throughout the session, keep your kindness and curiosity at the forefront. *"It seems hard for you to talk about that. What's it like to tell this story to me now?"* Respond to and normalize their emotions, but not by avoiding the topics at hand. *"I'm sorry it's so hard. It's difficult for a lot of people to share these things. I'm glad that you're telling me."*

"Nearly every new client is anxious about sharing their shortcomings, distress, and vulnerabilities with a stranger."

Goals

Ask clients what they want to be different when therapy has worked for them. Write down what they say, and translate, out loud, any negatives into positives and any passive wishes into active behaviors: "less anxious" becomes "more calm" and "my husband will be nice to me" becomes "I will deal differently with my husband." Ask them how they'll know when their goal has been reached, because it's lovely to program clients with certainty of a better, healthier, future. Ask enough questions to get a picture of how their problems are impacting them: *How often? How much of the time? Are there times or situations or certain people around whom this problem doesn't occur? How might you shift this from a negative to a positive statement, so we know where we're trying to go? How long has this been going on?* Here are some examples, including lists of client goals, the ultimate plan, and the length of therapy:

> "Ask enough questions to get a picture of how their problems are impacting them."

Woman, 28, anxiety and panic attacks

The 28-year-old anxious woman came in wanting to be less nervous. I began to diagnose her as she came through my door as a "skinny-nervous person," highly sensitive and wired for anxiety. As I did my assessment, she told me about frequent panic attacks, made self-deprecating statements, and in her response to my questions told me about her anxious/ disconnected mother and her history of "bad boyfriends." Here is the list of therapy goals we made at the end of the first session:

1. Less anxiety turns into: "be calmer"
2. Be free of panic attacks
3. Better relationships, including choosing a good boyfriend

4. More self-acceptance

5. More happiness

The Plan: relaxation and mindfulness skills, work on early attachment issues, ego state work to get her adult to take care of her child self and then pick the next boyfriend.

First, I taught her to interrupt her panic attacks by *breathing out all the way, then breathing in half-way, over and over.* This stops the hyperoxygenation that results from the getting ready to fight or flee bodily state.

Then I taught her Silencing the Alarm: *"Put your right hand near the top of your nose, run it over your left eyebrow, behind your ear, over the point of your shoulder, the point of your elbow, and off the back of your hand. . . Do this three times and switch hands to the other side and run it down your right side."* (This is from energy psychology, calming the "Triple Warmer" meridian. Stephen Porges saw me teach it and said it directly impacts and calms the vagus nerve.)

I suggested daily aerobics and a "slow" yoga class to burn off some steam and to learn to be in and to calm her body. In a few sessions, we had the panic attacks under control. She could stop them almost as soon as they started.

The attachment issues took longer. I connected closely with her, responding to every shift in affect and attention (CIMBS). We cleared early attachment disruptions and bad boyfriend interactions with EMDR. We did ego state work to connect the needy child in her to her functional, caring adult. And finally, we had her imagine evaluating potential boyfriends through her adult criteria: smart, sane, connectible, and solvent.

Eleven months later, she was calmer, rarely experiencing panic, and able to stop panic attacks when she was aware that she was good enough and that her shame was tied to the inadequate parenting she received. She was also dating a good guy who met the criteria she had established in therapy.

Woman, 23, survivor of a mass shooting, only a few previous traumas

Two days after the shooting, I saw the young woman who had witnessed many people being murdered. She and her family were untouched, but traumatized.

Here are her goals:

1. Sleep without nightmares, which became "Have good, uninterrupted sleep."
2. Stop having flashbacks, which became "Be in the present moment."
3. Stop looking for shooters everywhere, which became "Know I'm safe" and "Be alert without fear."
4. Gain trust of safety in the world again.
5. Get calm again.
6. Have joy again.

After checking her history (a few early distresses and recovery from an abusive boyfriend), we did immediate EMDR on the shooting, moving her from a Subjective Units of Distress Score (SUDS) of 10 down to a 2. During the next session we got her temporarily to 0, but she remained triggered by places that looked like the shooting site and anything that reminded her of it. After five sessions the incident was cleared, but memories of her abusive boyfriend arose. More EMDR. More connecting to now. Two months later, we were done!

Woman, 35, with a history of poor attachment and childhood abuse which gave her a mixed personality disorder

Sherri was difficult. She was so avoidant that she was often late for sessions. She would rattle on about her distress, but she rarely wanted to do the work to decrease it. And she constantly either idealized or demonized me, the therapist. Because she had deep shame that was hard for her to acknowledge and own, it was easier for her to say that I hated her than that she hated herself.

1. "Stop yelling at everyone" became "Learn to calm myself and speak nicely, even when there's conflict."
2. Be flashback-free.
3. Learn to tell the good people from the assholes and hang out with the good people.
4. Know that conflict doesn't mean someone hates me.
5. Know it's okay to say what I want, so I don't have to be a jerk about it.
6. Conquer avoidance. (Added later)

In our four years of therapy, she became able to tolerate sitting close, looking me in the eyes, being connected to me and to her feelings, noticing her feelings and not automatically acting on them, and using her most adult self to connect with younger, more avoidant parts. When she'd developed some affect tolerance, we used EMDR mixed with ego state therapy to heal the trauma of her emotional and physical abuse by her rage-filled parents. It took constant boundary setting and lots of patience on my part, but I had a transformed client at the end.

Man, 42, recovering from a major stroke

This therapy took six months. It included a lot of listening, some explanation of the grief process, and support for feeling everything.

Here are his goals:

1. Figure out who I am now and what I can do.
2. Deal with the fear of another stroke and my mortality.
3. Renegotiate the relationships I have with my wife and others.
4. Grieve the life and the brain that I used to have.

Like many stroke survivors, his emotions were very labile. The tears and rage both scared and embarrassed him. A lot of the work was on accepting and learning to channel all of his feelings. We included some couples therapy to help him and his wife decide what their relationship could be now. They both had very different roles, in both the day-to-day life and emotionally. We did a little EMDR on the moment of the stroke as well as the aftermath, which stopped the PTSD from intruding.

Man, 45, very depressed

Two years of therapy (including lots of ego state therapy, EMDR, and attachment-focused therapy), a referral for medication, and an exercise program. Here are his goals:

1. Be able to work again.
2. Feel better.
3. Have joy again.
4. Stop hating myself so much, which translated to "Accept and be kind to myself."
5. After more information: Clear out the effects of my rotten childhood, so it doesn't come back on me as more depression.

Therapy started with a referral to a psychiatrist for antidepressants. They helped some, but even with them, it took a lot of effort to connect with this depressed man. Once we did, we began working on his early childhood trauma and attachment deficits with ego-state therapy and EMDR, rescuing the child parts, bringing them to the present, and having the adult client and I give those young parts the love, support, connection, and attention that they always needed. In the meantime, I encouraged him to walk daily. And as his mood changed he added social activities, then a job. When his joy returned and his functioning was stable, we ended therapy, two years after we started.

Structure and Payment

Ideally you and your client find a time that is regular and fits perfectly into both of your schedules. If you work in an agency, you may not have control over your schedule, because the client books at the front desk. Your client may have an irregular work, school, or care-giving schedule that necessitates constant changes in timing. Whenever possible, set a regular time that creates a solid, predictable base for your future work.

Let your client know how long and how often your sessions will be. These metrics are often determined by the agency or insurance company that pays you. Standard sessions are forty-five to sixty minutes. Most people schedule weekly; however, psychodynamic therapists may schedule four sessions each week. Agencies that have too many clients or too few therapists may schedule them for one session every two or three weeks. Some clients (such as those that are highly dissociative, highly suicidal, or are currently experiencing terrible trauma) need the stability that can be gained from two or three sessions a week. And some therapists see people for "intensives," working several hours a day for a series of two to five days.

There are many ways to be paid for doing therapy. Your clients need to know how much, who is in charge of collection if it's not you, and how to communicate about it. If you work for an agency or some other employer, you may have nothing to do with collecting. If you don't work for an agency or other employer, you must decide if you'll have a cash-only practice, take insurance, or some combination of both. Some therapists have a set fee per session. Others have a sliding scale, depending on clients' abilities to pay. Set fees range from $50–200 per hour session. (The highest I've heard of was $400, in New York City.) If you are in private practice, you need to set a fee that is high enough to support yourself and low enough that it is reasonable for your region, expertise, and ability to attract and keep clients. When communicating with clients, be upfront about your fees and expectations. If you don't have a biller, you might use the first or last three minutes of each session to accept the client's check or credit card. There are now HIPAA-compliant online billing systems that hold credit card information, so you can automatically bill after each session.

Many therapists let their clients know that they charge for "no-shows" and/or less than twenty-four hours' notice of cancellation.

Let your clients know what they can expect the rhythm of the sessions to be: check-ins, therapy, payment, reschedule, and out the door by the end of the session. (Or check-in, therapy, and out the door to pay and reschedule at the front desk.)

At the end of the first session, your client should have an idea of their goals, a sense of how you might work together to achieve those goals, a sense of the structure of the sessions, a signed disclosure statement, and some connection with you.

Depending on the client's issues and ability to communicate, you may spend more sessions completing the history, honing the goals, and building the therapeutic relationship, before you tackle the gist of the problems. A highly dissociative client may not be able to tell you their history. A client who walks in the door and starts crying may not calm down enough to give you the information. Your job is to meet the clients where they are and direct them as much as you can.

Client Information Form:

Appointments are necessary for all sessions. I am available for emergency phone appointments. Emergency therapy appointments are dependent on schedule availability.

Contact me at _____ I check my messages at least two times each day, Monday through Friday. If you are having an emergency, please call my cell phone at _____ It may be several hours before I can return your call. You can call the Crisis Clinic at _____ if I cannot be reached. If you are in a life-threatening emergency, call 911.

Cancellations: You must give at least 24 hours advance notice for cancellations. I charge the full fee for missed appointments. If I can accommodate a last-minute change of schedule, I will. Otherwise, you will be charged if you cancel less than 24 hours before the session.

Fees: There is a charge for all scheduled appointments and all phone calls longer than 5 minutes. The current rate is $____ per 60-minute session, unless otherwise arranged. For sessions longer than 60 minutes, I will charge $___ per minute. Full payment is expected at each session, unless otherwise arranged.

You have the right to refuse treatment and to choose the provider and modality that best suits your needs. You have the right to say that you don't want to answer a question or use a specific particular modality at any time.

Insurance billing: Direct billing to your insurance company may be arranged. You are responsible for your co-payment at each session. You are responsible for all fees declined by your insurance company, unless otherwise arranged. You will not be responsible for a higher fee than I have negotiated with your insurance company.

Privacy Practices: Your heath record contains personal information about you and your health. State and federal law protects the confidentiality of this information. "Protected health information" (PHI) is information about you that may identify you or relate to your past, present, or future physical or mental health or health conditions and related health care services.

Confidentiality: As a client, you have a right to privacy. Generally, our discussions, clinical assessments, and records thereof are held as confidential communications. Written notes are secured in a locked file. Requests for acknowledgment of your participation or process in therapy will only be released with your informed and signed consent and only after being discussed with you. You may revoke your authorization at any time. There are, however, limits to confidentiality, guided by law and by clinical ethics.

1. When the client or another person is in a life-threatening situation, I must report to an appropriate authority to protect the person at risk.

2. If a client reports physically or sexually abusing a minor, an elder, or a developmentally disabled person of any age, I am required by law to report such abuse to state authorities. If clear, current threat of such abuse is present, I will take action to protect the individuals involved from additional abuse.

3. If a client is gravely disabled due to a mental disorder and a threat to themself or others and if that client refuses a recommendation of voluntary residential treatment, I will arrange for assessment by the state mental health professional team. If a client is an imminent threat to self or others, I may contact the police.

4. If you file suit against me or you commit a crime on my premises or against me, you waive your rights to privacy.

5. I may disclose your personal health information if it is required by law, such as for public health report notices and law enforcement reports. I also must make disclosures to the secretary of the Department of Health and Human Services if they are investigating or determining my compliance with the requirements of the Privacy Rule.

6. I may discuss you and your clinical situation with consultants to find the best way to assist you. In these cases, I will not disclose your name, place of work, or other clues to your identity.

7. I may use and disclose your PHI for the purpose of providing, coordinating, or managing your health care treatment and any related services. This may include coordination or management of your health care with a third party, consultation with other health care providers or referral to another provider for health care services. I will not use your PHI to obtain payment for your health

care services without your written authorization. Examples of payment-related activities are: making a determination of eligibility or coverage for insurance benefits, processing claims with your insurance company, reviewing services provided to you to determine "medical necessity," or undertaking utilization review activities.

8. I may use or disclose, as needed, your PHI to support the business activities of my professional practice. Such disclosures may be to others for health care education or to provide planning, quality assurance, peer review, administrative, legal, or financial service to assist the delivery of health care, provided I have a written contract that requires the recipients of the information to safeguard the privacy of your PHI. I may also contact to discuss appointment times or as arranged in a session.

9. If you believe that I have violated your privacy rights, you may file a complaint in writing to me at _____ Seattle, WA 98115. I will not retaliate against you for filing a complaint. You can choose to file a complaint with the Secretary of the Department of Health and Human Services and direct that complaint to him or her.

Confidentiality and insurance: Almost all insurances that pay for mental health benefits require periodic progress and process reports that become part of your permanent medical record. Minimally, a diagnosis is required. Often, reporting the goals of therapy and progress towards these goals is required. If you sign the standard insurance waiver of confidentiality, I, the therapist, must report whatever information your insurance company requests of me.

Online Communication: You may change appointments with me at my email or by text, but please send no personal or clinical information online, since email and texts are not secure media. If you send email from your employer's computer, your employer has legal access to it. Cell phones and cordless phones are not completely confidential, either. I never "friend" current or former clients on LinkedIn, Facebook, or any other social media.

Declining my services: I, the therapist, reserve the right to decline delivery of services and to provide a referral if I conclude that the continuance of therapy will be detrimental to the client or, in good faith, I judge that I am not adequately serving the client's best interests. I reserve the right to decline delivery of services to clients arriving at sessions intoxicated or "high" on alcohol or nonprescribed drugs and to decline subsequent services if this behavior continues. I reserve the right to expect nonexploitive and nonthreatening treatment from the client, to seek resolution, and if necessary, to decline services and seek appropriate intervention should exploitive treatment occur.

If you have a complaint or suspect I have shown unprofessional conduct, you may find my state's professional board workers code of ethics at or the state ethics codes at http://apps.leg.wa.gov/rcw/default.aspx?cite=18.130.180. You may contact _____ Office of Ethics and Professional Review for instructions on how to report any perceived violations. You may also file a complaint with the _____ state board of licensing: http://www._____

I have read and understood the above document.

Client's Name _____

Date signed _____

4 / **Assessment, Diagnoses, and Treatment Plans**

Diagnoses

Diagnoses are shorthand for the complex problems that most clients pose. There are several reasons to make a diagnosis. The most important reason is to help you and your client conceptualize the problem and then devise a roadmap for working through it. Most of the other reasons have to do with communication. If you're dealing with insurance companies, they want an ICD-10 diagnosis on which to base their payments. Your agency and other professionals who are treating the client need the shorthand of a diagnosis to make their decisions. Research is based on diagnoses: Does treatment X work better than treatment Y or a placebo?

The problem with many diagnoses is that they may not fit the client in front of you. First, clients often come in with more than one diagnosis. Someone with generalized anxiety may easily become traumatized and have traumatic stress, changing to post-traumatic stress, acute, changing to post-traumatic stress disorder, chronic. An individual with bipolar disorder may also have

"The problem with many diagnoses is that they may not fit the client in front of you."

borderline personality disorder. And many bipolar clients manifest their manic stages as some, or many, forms of anxiety disorders. Second, there are disorders we psychotherapists deal with daily that aren't written in the book. The most glaring lack is "complex trauma," or "attachment trauma" or "complex PTSD." Whatever you call it, it's the syndrome with foundations in repeated early trauma that results in chronic PTSD, attachment issues, depression, and various levels of dissociation. For insurance companies or people in the agency that review your paperwork, you'll put *F43.12 PTSD, Chronic.* For the client and people in your consultation group, you'll say *Complex Trauma* and they'll know what you mean. Every few years, a group of psychiatrists rework the diagnoses in the *Diagnostic Statistical Manual* (*DSM*), the bible of psychological diagnoses (American Psychiatric Association, 2013). And every year they leave out many of the syndromes that psychotherapists are treating.

Many diagnoses are useful, and it's worth your while to know how to use the DSM's multiaxial assessment of primary and personality diagnoses, general medical conditions, and psychosocial and environmental problems and also the Global Assessment of Functioning (GAF). The GAF is a 1–100 scale of function from 0—persistent danger of severely of hurting self or others or persistent inability to maintain minimal personal hygiene—to 100—superior function in a wide range of activities, life's problems never seem to get out of hand, sought out by others because of many positive qualities, no symptoms. The 100s never come to therapy. The 1–10s should be inpatients. And it's useful to know the list for good assessment of your new clients.

> "Many diagnoses are useful, and it's worth your while to know how to use the DSM."

Assessment

For you beginning therapists who might be overwhelmed with the magnitude of assessment data: don't worry. It gets easier as you go along. You already assess people every day. The more you know about psychology, the deeper and more automatic your assessments become. Experienced therapists can often get a broad idea of their clients' strengths and deficits in the first few minutes. They ask themselves: "Just how dissociated is this guy?" or "Is this an inborn anxiety disorder, a trauma reaction, or some of both?" and then look for the answers. The more knowledge and experience you have, the more these can inform your intuition and the more you know what to look for, what to ask, and what to skip in the assessment process.

Taking a History

My favorite way to begin to learn about clients is using genograms (family trees) with timelines of major life events running underneath. By asking questions and cocreating a map of the people, relationships, pathologies, connections (and lack thereof), and the major events of the client's life, you get to know the client and many of her or his issues quickly and in a form to which you can easily refer throughout the therapy. There are many online sites that sell applications for creating genograms. A great way to practice this technique is to create a genogram of your own family, which will help you learn the layout and the symbols. It is best to work with clients in the absence of a computer so that you can connect with them and it is also easier to share maps on paper than on a computer screen. I like to use a handful of colored pens and a large sheet of paper in full view of both of us and on which we can make corrections and additions. We start the map construction by writing in the immediate family: spouses, children, exes, siblings, parents, step-parents, half- and step-siblings, including the client's relationship to each of them. We chart affection, support, abuse, and estrangements. In the meantime, we find out where everyone lives, what they do, who they're married to, and what they do and don't share with the client: Alcoholism or other addictions? Depression? Bipolar disorder? Anxiety? Obesity? Familial diseases? A love of sport, profession, or hobbies?

Next, we assess earlier generations. Where were the parents, the grand-parents, and the greats born? In what social class? What was their culture? Their religion (if any)? The family trauma or secret? Who is still around? Who has died or become estranged, and how did that impact the client? And what relationship does your client have with each of them now, and what was their relationship in the past?

Maureen Kitchur's (2005) trauma-informed model of genograms includes red arrows from abusers to victims, labeled with *s* for sexual abuse, *p* for physical abuse, and *e* for emotional abuse. Many models include coding for illness, mental illness, addictions, and other family traits. It can be useful for clients to visualize the generations of abuse, anxiety disorders, systemic oppression, or codependence to understand the context of their problems. One helpful book is *Genograms: Assessment and Intervention* (McGoldrick, Gerson, & Petry, 2008).

Other questions to consider: Who were other influential people, for better or worse, outside of the family? Best friends? Favorite teachers, coaches, friends' parents? Abusive people from anywhere? Bullies? Favorite supportive groups, then and now? Is the client part of a group, by virtue of race, class, ethnicity, religion, or disability, that is singled out for separation, abuse, or distressing societal projection? And what is the configuration of current life: work, family, friends, groups, religious institutions, hobbies, beloved pets, joys, fears?

Throughout this mapping process, you'll have been adding traumas, life changes, wins, moves, and other events to the timeline at the bottom, and asking the client, *"What am I missing?"* Within a session or two, you will have a comprehensive sense of the client's life, a list of traumas to clear, and (hopefully) a list of remembered resources. Up to this point, you have indeed been creating a diagnosis and planning the direction of the rest of therapy; however, there's more to assess.

Social Cues

In any contact, from the first phone call on, you are watching your clients closely. Look for social cues: Is there easy eye contact? Are the client's eyes downcast, which might connote shame, depression, or simply shyness? Is the client able to participate in regular back and forth communication? Does the client express any humor: for connection or defense? Does the client seem to be afraid of you? Express defiance? Defensiveness? (See Chapter 9, Healing Attachment Wounds.) Is the client able to correct you assertively if you get something wrong or is he or she too deferential? Does the client display aggression if you get too close? Or if they feel too much, do they exhibit attachment and/or affect intolerance? Is the client desperate for your approval and terrified of what you might think, which would indicate insecure attachment?

Temperament

We are born with distinct temperaments. We are predisposed to be night owls or early risers, introverts or extroverts, stolidly calm or reactively nervous. People can be born with predispositions for depression, anxiety, or bipolar disorder. These conditions as well as our less pathological temperaments predict some of our perceptions and responses to trauma, attachment breaches, and everyday irritations. Notice how your clients' inborn temperaments impact the issues they bring.

- How does this client seem? Nervous? Calm? Depressed? Spaced out?
- Is he a skinny, nervous person? (Generalized anxiety disorder or highly sensitive person; Aron, 1996)
- Is she hypervigilant about your response to her? (Social anxiety)
- Is he sitting like a lump? (Depression, illness, exhaustion, dissociation)
- Does she avoid different subjects, going on at length about the minutiae of unrelated things? (Obsessive-compulsive, obsessive-

compulsive personality, or attention deficit disorder or just plain avoidance)

- Does he change the subject every few seconds? (Mania, attention deficit disorder, and/or avoidance)
- Are there any other signs of major depression, mania, or anxiety disorders?

Questions for the Client

- *You seem a little anxious. Is that normal for you, did it start with the car accident, or is it because of this therapy situation?*
- *How far back can you remember being anxious/depressed?*
- *Have you ever had a panic attack? When was the first one? What are they like?*
- *Have you ever taken medications for anxiety/depression? What kind?*
- *Are you still taking medications? How are they working?*
- *Is there anyone else in your family who has anxiety/depression? What are they like?*
- *Any depression, bipolar, or manic depression in your family? Any schizophrenia?*
- *Has anyone in your family been hospitalized for emotional issues? Taken medications? Do you know what kind?*
- *Have you had any of these diagnoses?*
- If pertinent: *How long have you been anxious, depressed, or feeling angry? Did the feelings start after the traumatic event, or have you felt that way for a long time? Do the feelings come and go, or hang around all the time?*

Culture

Everyone is born into a cultural context. We all have a race, an ethnicity, a social class, a gender, and a sexual orientation. Some of us fit into our expected niches. Many of us don't.

Know who you're dealing with. And watch out for your own projections about who your clients are. Acknowledge (to yourself) your biases and prejudices about the person with whom you're working. Then work to know more about your particular client. Be aware of the chronic trauma that dysfunctional sex role expectations, directed hatred, institutionalized discrimination, and social expectations can have on individuals who don't fit the dominant picture of how they're supposed to be.

While you're doing your other assessments, keep these things in mind:

- Culture: What kind of cultural and familial expectations does your client hold? What is the client's dominant feeling? Pride? Shame? Fear of being hurt, rejected, beaten up, shunned, never measuring up, or loved only if he or she fits in, without being truly seen?
- Social class: Did the family fit into their milieu? Was there a change in social class for the family or the client? How did that affect your client? Did your client fit in? What were the class-based expectations? For example, "We must always look perfect"? "We'll never amount to anything"?
- Race: Were there chronic stressors tied to race? Specific discrete traumas? What were the family's expectations? The neighborhood's? The culture's?
- Migration: Where did your client come from? Was the move traumatic? Was the client fleeing discrimination, economic hardship, or genocide in her or his original culture? Is there a disconnect between social expectations in the homeland and this culture? Does your client feel like an integral part of this society? How long did that take? Or: How many generations has the family been in this country? How and when did they get here?
- Sexual orientation: Is he or she "out"? Scared to tell the family? Are

there constant fears of being discovered or being discounted? Has the client experienced discreet traumatic incidents? Bashing? Does the client have a supportive family and a happy gay relationship that has nothing to do with the trauma that brought her or him to therapy?

- Gender: Does he fit the stereotype of a "real man"? Does she fit the expectation of a female in her culture? What did it cost this client to try to fit in or to remain so different? Were there lower expectations because she was a girl? Is there gender dysphoria (the sense that she or he was born in the wrong body), or does the client float fluidly in between genders? Do they prefer different pronouns (they, ze)? What kinds of discrimination and harassment has she, he, or they run into? In what ways are gender expectations keeping the client from full self-acceptance?

- Religion: What did religion tell your client about him or herself? Did its message induce trauma? Offer solace and support? Provide a strong sense of values? Engender a sense of a supportive deity? Was there discrimination? An impossible standard to live up to? Did the client feel a strong identification with the community? Was there no religion or spirituality in the client's life? Is there spirituality of any kind in the client's current life? (Make sure that you avoid any hint of proselytizing!)

- Appearance: Do they feel self-hatred for their body type or appearance? Do they think that their body is all they have? Have they been humiliated for being too slight to play football? Is there anything unusual about the client's appearance? Is it intentional?

- Disability: How did other people treat this disability? Did it make your client feel separate? If so, how? What impacts has this had on your client's life? Is there grief related to the disability or its impacts?

- Family: What were the family's messages about self, about the larger society, and about being enough? Do "The Smiths never give up"? Do they always fail? Does the client feel safe in and fully part of the family? Is the client estranged from or seen as the different one in or the caretaker of the family? Was the family a dangerous place to be? Is there estrangement from certain members or the whole bunch?

- Which answers to these questions tweak you with regard to this client? What projections do you need to keep in check so that you may truly see the client in front of you? What kind of research do you need to do about this client's culture or situation? And how do you keep yourself from blindly laying what you learn onto a client for whom it may not fit?

Attachment and Affect Regulation

Our brains are predisposed to learn how to regulate our emotions. Our interactions with caregivers are where that learning takes place (Siegel, 1999; Schore, 1994). When our parent or caregiver mirrors our affect, soothes us, or responds appropriately to us, we learn that we can expect a response, that we are worth responding to, and that we can be soothed. During this time, we build the neural hardware for handling our emotions. If our caregiver is depressed, addicted, overwhelmed, angry, or absent, we might learn that help is unreliable or unavailable, that we aren't worthy of being helped, and that we don't have good ways to calm down. Without the brain hardware for calming down, some people learn to reflexively dissociate when emotions—even pleasant emotions—arise. They come to be at the mercy of every emotion that runs through them, either dissociating or overreacting to strong affect, whether positive or negative. (Think about histrionic or borderline personality disorders, who may scream, cry, or run, when emotions are triggered.) If this happens over and over, these experiences build and strengthen the hardware for strong state-specific reactions and poor or nonexistent self-regulation.

People with poor affect regulation react strongly to distress and may have stronger and more pernicious PTSD symptoms from newer trauma. Poor attachment accompanies early abuse and physical neglect—watch for bone-deep trauma reactions (including dissociation) in people with disordered attachment.

Attachment Assessment

Observation

- Can this client connect? Make eye contact?
- Does she respond appropriately to me? To humor? To serious inquiry?
- Is his narrative coherent when he's talking about childhood? How is his narrative not holding together? (Mary Main [1991] found that coherency of narrative in discussing childhood was the strongest indication of attachment style and level of dissociation.)
- How do I feel in the presence of this person? Comfortable? Defensive? Distant? Connected? (This is often a reflection of what's going on in the client.)
- As she talks about her life, does she seem like her actual age or younger? Does it feel like she's switching from one neural network (age or part) to another?
- Is she trying to take care of me? Is she asking too many questions about me? Is it possible that the caregiver is the only role she knows?

Questions for the Client

- What was your family going through when you were a kid? Any deaths, miscarriages, losses, divorces, moves, big changes? What was the effect of these changes on your parents? On you?
- Who took care of you? One parent? Both? Paid caregivers? Relatives? No one? What was that like?
- How did your family deal with feelings?
- What happened when you cried? Got mad? Needed something? Ran around making noise?
- Was there anyone who made you feel treasured or adored?
- Was there anyone who made you feel like you weren't wanted? That

you shouldn't have been born? That you were too much to deal with? (Check out older siblings with this question.)

- What was your role in your family? Were you the troublemaker, caregiver, family hero, scapegoat, invisible one? (Shapiro, 2010, pp. 33).

Affect Tolerance

The Window of Tolerance

Traumatized, anxious, and/or poorly attached people are vulnerable to hyperarousal or mobilized states. *Hyper*arousal may include increased sensation, emotional reactivity, hypervigilance, intrusive imagery, and disorganized cognitive processing. *Hypo*arousal or immobilized states show numbed sensation and emotion, disabled cognitive processing, and reduced physical movement (Ogden et al., 2006). Between these autonomic zones lies the window of tolerance (Ogden et al., 2006), the optimal arousal zone from which people experience "various intensities of emotional and physiological arousal without disrupting the functioning of the system" (Siegel, 1999, p. 253). Therapists must assist clients to stay in their window of tolerance so they can think, feel, and process through their traumas without becoming overwhelmed or shut down. Early in therapy, therapists need to assess their clients' range of and tolerance for affect and autonomic states. Throughout the therapy, therapists need to collaborate with their clients to keep them in their window of tolerance: where they are able to think, feel, and process their emotions.

Affect Tolerance Assessment

Observation

- Is their affect appropriate to the material?
- Do they space out or freak out when a feeling begins to arise?

- Are they embarrassed by showing feeling? (Is this a gender issue, "Boys don't cry"; family training to "buck up"; or something else?)
- Can they tolerate their positive affect? Smile? Laugh appropriately? Feel pride?
- What is their window of tolerance for affect? What amount of affect or arousal causes them to shut down or get too distressed?
- Is there just one affect the client lives in? Anger, irritation, anxiety, teasing humor, suspicion, or defensiveness?

Questions for the Client

- *What's it like to cry now? Do you cry? Does it feel manageable, like you can stop if you want to? Do you feel ashamed to cry?* (Watch for gender and cultural differences here.)
- If there was a recent trauma:
  - *How have your feelings changed since the event?*
  - *What were your feelings like before the event?*
  - *When you think of what happened or get triggered, do you ever feel shut down?* (Check for depression, too.)
  - *When you think of what happened or get triggered, do you ever feel so agitated you can't stand it?*

- *Describe a time when you felt proud of yourself. What do you feel in your body when you think of that?* (If they can't think of a proud time, consider attachment problems. If they can think of a time but can't feel it now, it could be PTSD-related or depression.)
- *What happens when you get mad? Can you express it? Do you feel in control of yourself when you're angry? Does it feel safe to be angry?*
- *Have you ever experienced a big loss? Tell me about it.* (Watch for appropriate or inappropriate affect.)

Dissociation Assessment

It's easy to diagnose dissociative identity disorder (DID) when your client of several sessions changes stance and voice and asks, "Who are you? Where is this? What are we doing here?" (Showing huge –state changes and obvious amnesia between states.) Most signs of dissociation are subtler. The more you know about dissociation, the more you automatically watch for its markers, such as your new client:

1. Spaces out easily
2. Loses coherency when speaking about childhood events (Main, 1991; Siegel, 1999)
3. Can't remember much of their childhood years
4. Begins to use different voices, inflections, or age-specific language
5. Abruptly switches from calm discussion to a hostile, terrified, shut down, or disorganized state
6. Is easily triggered into feelings of abandonment, defensiveness, or clinginess
7. Subtly or not so subtly changes stance and expression in a "weird" way
8. Has otherwise unexplained headaches or pelvic pain
9. Doesn't connect with you
10. Shows inappropriate affect when discussing distressing events— smiling or no evidence of feeling at all.
11. Speaks in the third person about themself
12. Forgets appointments, despite a good therapeutic relationship

Since few clients announce that they have secondary dissociation (personality or "character" disorders), DID, or DDNOS (tertiary dissociation), some clinicians use diagnostic tools to screen every client for dissociative disorders. Others use these tools only when they can't come to a diagnosis without them.

Here are some helpful screening tools:

1. The Dissociative Experiences Scale (DES) is a 28-item questionnaire on which the client reports on the prevalence of common and not-so-common dissociative experiences. It's easily rated for degrees of dissociation from PTSD to DID (Bernstein & Putnam, 1986).

2. The Dissociative Disorders Interview Schedule (DDIS) is a comprehensive, 132-item, highly structured interview. It evaluates depression, borderline personality disorder, and all levels of dissociation. Download it (for free) at https://www.rossinst.com/ddis from Dr. Colin Ross (1997), its creator. Just by reading it, you will become a better diagnostician.

3. Somatoform Dissociation Questionnaire (SDQ): Available in 20-item and 5-item versions, the SDQ evaluates somatoform dissociation (physical and sensory experiences) and other dissociative disorders.

4. The Multidimensional Inventory of Dissociation (MID) developed by Paul Dell (https://www.mid-assessment.com).

You'll find more information on diagnoses in later chapters.

Treatment Plans

Once you've done your assessments, figured out your client's diagnosis, and agreed with your client on the goals of therapy, it's time to make a plan. If you are wedded to only one therapy technique, you may have the same plan for every client. If you know more than one technique, you may look at each client through the lenses of several therapies to determine where to start and what to do next. Clients with multiple diagnoses may require complex plans. Here are some of the usual components of treatment plans, in the order in which you would work through them. Many of these may run concurrently.

> *"Clients with multiple diagnoses may require complex plans."*

1. Establish the safety and positive regard of the therapeutic relationship.
2. Make goals together.
3. Stabilize the clients, if needed
   a. Make sure they're in a safe living environment and know it.
   b. Orient them to present safety.
   c. Make sure they have the basic skills to navigate their internal and external world.
   d. If they need medication or other medical interventions, make appropriate referrals. A highly manic, psychotic, or severely depressed client will not respond well to most therapeutic interventions alone. Make sure you refer to an expert in psychiatric medications. Most general practitioners don't have the appropriate expertise. And make sure the psychiatrist or nurse practitioner is one who will communicate with and work with you.
   e. Help dissociated or traumatized clients bring the most adult and capable parts of themselves to the front for better functioning in today's world.

Explain the course of treatment in the context of the client's goals:

    a. For OCD or GAD: *"We'll be working on managing your anxiety. Since it seems that you don't have a lot of trauma to clear out, we'll be working on ways to calm your body and pull your brain away from those repetitive thoughts. Expect to learn a bunch of good tools to bring down that anxiety. And expect that you'll be seeing me for a few months."*

    b. For that rare one-time occurrence of PTSD: *"I think we can clear that trauma out of your body and brain using EMDR/ego state therapy/somatic therapy/etc. in a few sessions/a few months."*

    c. For people with poor attachment histories, poor or dysfunctional current relationships, and (often) personality disorders: *"With the kind of childhood you had, you didn't get some of the good wiring you need to thrive. We're going to build some new wiring by how we relate here, by examining what works and what doesn't in your current ways of relating, and by teaching you some new skills. We'll also work directly with that early trauma, and clear its effects. Expect to be seeing me for a few years to complete this rewiring."*

    d. For people with disastrous early trauma and attachment, with diagnoses of DID or other serious dissociation, if you know how to treat them: *"We've got a lot of work to do. First, we're going to find the parts of you that are up front in your day-to-day life (the mom part, the working part, the part that knows how to balance your accounts) and put those parts up front to keep your life running smoothly. Then we'll help all the other pieces of you orient to the present, know they're safe, and be able to let the grown-up parts run the show. After that, we'll work to heal all parts of you, clearing the effects of all traumas so that all of you is healed. You'll be a much more connected, and possibly more singular, you. This is going to take a while, probably some years, and I'm committed to being here for all parts of you throughout this process.*

e. For people with disorders that you don't yet know how to work with and can't get the education you need, or if you have plans (brief internship, impending retirement, etc.) that would prevent you from committing to the full duration of treatment: *"I wish that I could work with you, but I'm not going to be in practice long enough to do the work you need. (Or, I don't have the skills I would need to serve you well.) Jane Doe has these skills and/or will be in practice long enough to get you where you want to be. I've already contacted her, and she's ready to take you on once you call her. When you do, may I give her all the information I've gathered about you, so that she doesn't have to ask you the same questions again?*

Begin to implement your plan. (The rest of this book!)

5 / **Sessions**

By the end of the first session, or first few sessions, you have (hopefully) connected with the client, discussed goals, made your initial assessment, and discussed your treatment strategies for meeting the agreed upon goals. The disclosure statements have been signed, and the client is in your schedule. What's next?

Some of what's next depends on your client's goals. And some of what's next is so important that it must be done in every session. The most important thing is maintaining connection with your client in a way that they recognize:

> *"Make sure that you are absolutely present."*

1. Make sure that you are absolutely present. Be grounded, be rested, and be aware of what distress and discomfort (grief, anxiety, illness) may be going on for you; put them aside, and bring your attention fully into the room for your client.
2. Watch your client like a hawk. Notice your client's feeling states, thought process, degree of connection with you, and of course, notice the content of what your client communicates.

3. Respond to your client with empathy and curiosity. Responses can be anything from a nod to a high five. Let the client know that you hear what they're saying and also, that you're seeing, and maybe feeling, them:

   a. *"Tell me more about _____."*

   b. You may notice how your body feels or is mirroring the client's body and respond to that: *"When you started talking about that, your body seemed to get tense. What are you feeling now?"*

   c. From Object Relations Therapy, when you start feeling the client's disowned or dissociated affect (the feelings that they reflexively ignore or push down) in your body: *"There's some anger in the room. Do you know anything about that?"*

   d. From Diana Fosha's (2000) wonderful AEDP therapy: *"What's it like for you to know how sad and angry I am that you were abused like that?"* Or, *"What's it like for you to know how happy I feel that that's happening for you?"* (You use this to let clients consider that they are, in fact, making an impression on you. This especially helpful with people with poor attachment.)

Most clients can be gently steered toward their goals using the following prompts:

- *"We did a big piece of work last week. What have you been noticing since then? When you think about it, what do you notice now?"*
- *"I'm loving this story, and I'm afraid we'll run out of time before we get to _____, today. Will you be ready to go after the trauma/anxiety/ etc.?"*
- *"Let's check in and get back to _____."*
- *"What's next on our list?"*

For clients, especially anxious and/or traumatized ones, who are avoidant or even have a phobia of approaching the material, you may turn up both the containment and the heat:

- *"It's really hard to think about that hard stuff, and much easier to talk about X. But are you willing to approach that awful incident with me? I'll be with you every minute."*
- *"I know you have a lot of feelings about X. Let's get you as grounded as you can be before those big feelings can run through you. Look around. Are you safe right here and right now? Can you feel gravity holding you in that chair? Feel your feet on the floor and feel the air going into your lungs. Now let's approach the stuff you came in here to deal with."*

The content of the middle part of the session will depend on what the goals are, who the client is, and where you are in the therapy process. Whatever the goal, stay connected, responsive, and curious; remain on track and balance goals and connection in every moment. If the goal is connection, that's easy. Guide clients' attention back to the relationship with statements such as *"Bring your attention right here to us, and as you look over here, notice what's happening in your body."* Or *"What just happened?"*

If you're working on another goal (clearing trauma, bringing mindfulness, or solving a problem) you can

> **"Different clients need different responses."**

continually let the client know that you're present and connected by your responses. Different clients need different responses. Some just need to catch your gaze. Others need you to voice your response, *"I see how hard that is for you."* Or *"Good job!"* Or for the ones who can't imagine anyone caring, in the style of Diana Fosha, *"What's it like for you to know how sad I am that that happened to you?"*

Time Keeping

Start sessions on time. It's important that your clients can trust you to maintain the structure of therapy. People who came from chaotic backgrounds may be watching you closely to see if your word is reliable. If you're more than a minute late for a session, apologize. I tell my clients that if they're waiting for longer than five minutes, they should knock on the door to see if I'm in, aware of the time, and have not accidentally gotten my schedule confused. Occasionally, the clients or I have the wrong day. Fix any problems, and apologize if it's your fault.

In the (hopefully rare) case that you have to run over with the client before, make contact with the next client before their session is scheduled to start, let them know it's an emergency and how long it will be before you'll be able to call them in. I do this about once a year.

During each session, keep an eye on the clock. Time-keeping is important so that when the time comes to walk out your door, your client is fully present, grounded, and ready to face the world. The more dissociative the client is, the more time you may need for orientation and reconnection to the present. Some clients will try to extend their sessions with the infamous "doorknob communications," telling you something important in the last minute. *"Let me write that down so we can deal with it in next week's session,"* is a good way to cope with these instances.

If a client initiates many doorknob chats, bring it up as the avoidance or attachment issue it is. It might be that the client has avoided the main topic until the end. Early in your sessions, ask, *"Are we avoiding a big topic? Go inside, and see if there is something we need to focus on."* If the client's behavior stems from not wanting to leave, develop a ritual: *"It's hard to leave. What do you feel when it's the end of the session? Imagine you're leaving right now. What do you feel? What do you need? What age goes with that? Let's try this today. Right before the end, we will have your most adult part get in touch with the little one who doesn't want to leave, ask her to turn that kid around, look her in the eyes, and let her know that you, the adult, will be taking care of her all week and that you will remind her that she gets to see me again next Thursday."*

6 / **Ethics, Boundaries, and Transference Issues**

Boundaries make therapy possible. The roles of therapist and client are, and should be, sacred. Boundaries define your job as the helper, connector, and rule-setter, and the client's job as the one who gets the attention and the intended help and healing. You will have many opportunities to demonstrate what the boundaries are and, sometimes, to discuss them. Let's look at the most basic boundaries:

- You're being paid a set fee for giving your client your full attention for a set period of time. The therapy hour is not about you!
- Clients are paying you for that set time only. They don't get to call you when they feel lonely, have a big feeling, have a new idea, or just really want to talk. (Imagine if you had twenty people a week calling you at whim.) Exceptions to this boundary can be made in rare times of crisis or for a predetermined communication. Some exceptions might include, *"I can't get the suicide thoughts out of my head!"* Or, *"My mom made it through the surgery okay."*
- Your clients are not there to take care of you. Some of them were raised to take care of everyone, and you'll have to sweetly and as-

sertively bring them back to focus on themselves. *"I'm good, and I want to know how* you're *doing."* And if this keeps happening, *"What's going on inside when you start asking about me? Is there a feeling or topic we're avoiding?"*

- You are the time-keeper. Expect (train) your clients to come on time and leave on time. With disorganized clients, you might have them set alarms for when they need to get ready to come to session. Start winding down before the last minute and leave time to deal with money and scheduling. Most clients won't have a problem with this. Some of the more regressed ones will attempt to prolong appointments with the infamous "doorknob communications," starting an important topic just as the session is ending. Sometimes they've avoided telling you something during the session because it's painful, but in the end they realize that they need to tell you. Some may be trying to stay in the room. Either way, you need to let them know that you're writing it down and they must wait to talk about it at the next session.

- It's none of your clients' business if you're attracted to them or if you want them to be your best friend. It *is* your business to figure out what's going on. Yes, some people are inherently adorable, but there's often something else happening when you, the therapist, get turned on in a session. The big question to ask yourself is "Is it you, or is it them?" And then follow these leads:
  - Am I particularly lonely or lacking connection in my personal life?
  - Am I throwing my need at this client and provoking a response?
  - Am I picking up on something about the client? Do they habitually use sexual or social seduction to connect to others? Is this a normal defense mechanism this person uses to cope with close interactions? (Every time I'd feel a sexual feeling around a male client with a sex addiction, I'd say, *"I feel the vibe in the room. What feeling are we avoiding right now?"* His answer was always

anxiety, shame, or grief. The minute he felt the underlying emotion, the sexual vibe left the room.

- Is there normally a great therapeutic connection with mutual delight on both sides to be simply enjoyed?
- Is the client falling in love with me because this therapy is the most intimate, warm, and connected relationship they have? In that case, if the client tells me that they're in love with me, I say something like, *"That's great! Clients are supposed to fall in love with their therapists! From what you've told me, you've never gotten attachment attention from anyone else. Love is the right thing to call that feeling of trust, connection, and delight that bounces back and forth. And it's safe love, because it will never leave this room. We're rewiring your brain to be able love someone who's got your back and to enjoy the experience of good connection, unlike in your rotten childhood. When you're farther along in therapy, you're going to be able to connect with someone who is available, outside this room, for your good love!"*

Transference and Countertransference Issues

In a normal psychotherapy, you and your client will have affection for each other. You will closely monitor each other's mood and responses. You will care about what happens to each other. You may both feel delight upon meeting again. Often, you will feel your client's emotions inside your own body, before they have expressed them. What could possibly go wrong?

1. Clients project their stuff onto you
   a. New clients are often fearful of the judgements that you may have of them. They will watch you, apprehensively, for any sign of disapproval. If you notice this, you can ask them about it

and clear up the projection: *"I'm here to support you, not judge you. Any time you worry about how I'm seeing you, please tell me about it, and we can clear that up."* Clients that you have had for a while may still project the shame they feel onto you. Keep letting them know that they are sensing their feelings about themselves, not yours.

b. While it lasts, enjoy the projection of perfection and complete goodness that you get from some clients. You may be the only person in some clients' lives who gives them support, caring, and understanding. And often there is real caring and real love that bounces between clients and therapists. Some clients will hold onto their idealization of you through the whole course of therapy. Many will start seeing you as a regular person. Some, often clients with personality disorders, will start out idealizing you and then project diabolical intentions on you. Expect it and talk about it. *"Can you notice the feelings you're having about me now? What emotion is up right now? What happened here that brings that up? I wonder if you can hold the way you thought about me last week at the same time as the feelings you're having right now. I wonder, who was the last person you felt this way about?"*

> **"You may be the only person in some clients' lives who gives them support, caring, and understanding."**

c. Clients with abusive or highly critical parents or partners may project those behaviors on you. When they do, help them to notice and then to differentiate you from that other person. *"Try to put your highly critical mother and how she treated/treats you in one hand. In the other, put me and how I treat you. . . Notice the difference. Let's sit here, with how I am and how she was, and process those emotions"* (Shapiro, 2005b).

d. Some clients will try to argue with any- or everything you say.

These clients had to develop a defense against the people around them. Keep bringing them back to the feeling they're currently having, the situations where the feelings first arose, and the relative safety of you and your office. Try not to take this personally!

2. Therapists' self-disclosure

   a. If you want to talk about anything personal to you, ask yourself, *"Is it for me or is it for the client?"* (Di Donato, 2019). Some clients end up knowing way too much about their therapists because of the therapists' need to be seen. You might use an example to normalize a situation: *"Oh, yeah, I do that all that time. So does everyone."* But watch out for storytelling or looking for support from your client. You may briefly disclose a reason for a canceled session, but don't launch into a detailed story.

3. Attachment turns to attraction: Your client is attracted to you

   a. The closest and most intimate relationship the client has may be the one with you. Sometimes such clients will develop sexual feelings for you. When this happens, and they disclose it, accept the feelings like every other feeling and let them know what the boundaries are: *"Every emotion that you have is welcome here. It makes sense that you're feeling that, since we've gotten so close in our work together. Our relationship cannot go outside of this room, nor can it ever be sexual. And working through this can be very helpful."*

   b. With socially isolated or avoidant clients: *"It seems that you haven't felt this way about anyone for a long time. It's lovely that you feel safe and connected enough to feel that here with me. Our job is to get you to the place where you can feel that for someone who is appropriate and available. Let's talk about what it's like to feel that and then talk about that here."*

   c. And with clients whose biggest defense is sexualizing everyone: *"It's perfect that you're feeling that with me! We can work with this right here and now. Close your eyes and go inside and find the emotion that triggered this sexual feeling. Anxiety? Perfect. Let's hang out with that feeling for a while and see what it's about."*

4. You are attracted to a client
   a. Admit it to yourself and someone else. It's not unusual. You're in an intimate relationship with this person. They might be attractive. Or you might be picking up on their unspoken, or spoken, attraction to you. By telling someone else, especially a good consultant, a colleague, and/or your significant other, you're building a wall of protection around that client. And you're normalizing a normal thing. Yes, we become attracted to people that we're close to.
   b. Don't tell the client. It's not their job to deal with your feelings.
   c. If you're picking up on a client's sexual feelings, let it be "grist" for therapeutic mill: *"I'm noticing a feeling in the room. What's happening in you?"* This often happens with sexually compulsive clients. Don't take it personally. They do this with everyone, and it is often completely unconscious.
   d. If you find yourself obsessed with a client, get help immediately. Find a good therapist who can help you deal with your compulsion. Find out what kind of early issue you are projecting onto the client, and get help with it. If it gets in the way of your ability to provide good therapy, you'll need to refer the client to another good therapist. Never intrude on their life.
   e. There are therapists who step way over the sexual boundary and have sexual or romantic relationships with clients. It is your job to report this to their professional association. Some of these people are predators. Some of them are simply not in control of their needs. It's never okay. It's illegal in every state and forbidden in every therapeutic profession. And it exploits the safety and closeness that should be the basis of every therapeutic interaction.

5. You are traumatized by a client's trauma

   a. If you're having flashbacks or bad dreams about a client's trauma, that's secondary trauma, which is real PTSD. First, normalize it. Therapists often hear horrible stories, and it affect us. You're not abnormal. Your empathy connects you to your client's pain. Make sure you have good support from a good consultant or consultation group. If the horrible stories persist, get some good trauma therapy for yourself, and clear them. Make sure you have good therapy tools to clear the client's trauma. Often, secondary trauma goes away when the client's trauma is cleared. If your distress persists even after the client heals, pursue good trauma therapy for yourself.

6. You want to take all the pain away, immediately, and feel shame that you can't

   a. It's okay to feel grief about your client's pain and to grieve that you can't immediately take it away. It's okay to recognize that you don't have the tools to help someone, at which time you may think about a referral to someone who does. When you feel shame about not helping quickly enough, look to your own issues. A younger part of you, who "failed" to fix some other person or problem, may be "up" and in need of some recognition and forgiveness.

   "Make sure you have good support from a good consultant or consultation group."

7. You are tempted to try to help the client outside of sessions, run late with them, or call them because you're worried about them

   a. In these cases, you must assess the needs of your client and your own need to help. Some clients, especially highly dissociated, traumatized, or psychotic ones, need longer or more frequent sessions. In that case, schedule them and keep to that schedule. Sometimes clients can trigger our own need to fix things or our own distress. Use your consultant, colleagues, and possibly your own therapy to figure out how to contain your distress and give your client what they need—within proper boundaries.

8. Your client calls or texts you several times a day, whenever they're distressed
   a. This is an affect tolerance issue and possibly dissociation. Let them know, in session, that you cannot respond to all their calls and texts, nor can you see them outside of sessions. Then work with them to help them identify the affect or part of them that drives them to call you, and use the calm-down and containment techniques you'll find in Chapter 8, Building Affect Tolerance. With more dissociated clients, you'll need to do ego state work to put the most grownup parts of the client in charge and calm the young ones, who would rather have you than their own grown-up selves.

      If you respond to every out-of-session request that a borderline or DID client makes, you become, in effect, a "part" of your client. It's much better for them to have an internal adult-caregiver 24/7 than an irritated or overwhelmed therapist. If they absolutely can't find that adult part, have them imagine the perfect caregiver in the healing place. (See Chapter 9, Healing Attachment Wounds.) You may have to go several rounds with this issue, as the young parts want *you*, not their own adult, to do the caregiving. Use it to fully explore the desperation of those young, distressed parts.

9. Touching clients
   a. Touch is complex and includes issues of gender, sexuality, and both the client's and the therapist's boundaries.

- Some touch is simple: a high-five when the client has attained an important goal to share the delight of that win, or reciprocating when the client extends his arm to shake hands at the end of a good session.
- Some therapies include touch. EMDR therapists may tap on their clients' hands or knees. Somatic therapists may have their clients push against their hands. It's important to check out the touch each time. *"Is it okay if I tap on you now?"* or *"You want to push these hands?"* Watch carefully to see if you're getting automatic compliance or true informed consent.
- Hugging can be complex. It should never be an expectation from the therapist. It must be initiated by the client and often should be discussed beforehand. Some therapists, especially men, have a no hugging rule. Here are some scenarios and how you might deal with them:
  - Female therapist, female client, no sexual attraction, client wants to hug goodbye at end of session, and client shows no sign of regression: Do it. Hold on only as long as the client does.
  - Same configuration as above, but client is regressed. Talk about hugs with the client. What's happening and what parts of the client want a hug and what parts may not. Say, *"I want to hug the adult part of you, and have your adult part bring the hug to the little girl that's inside."* You're taking yourself out of the caregiver role and giving that to the client's most functional part. You're helping bring the adult up to deal with the world outside your office.
  - Male therapist, female or male client with a history of sexual abuse by men. Client may obediently hug from a regressed state, feeling compelled to obey as they did as a child. Address it this way: *"I want to hold off on hugging until we both know that you are reaching out from your*

most adult part and you know, absolutely, that you never have to touch me. You know I care for you. I don't want to harm you in any way. Let's do an air hug, right now. When you're more healed, we can hug if you want to."

- Codependent client who always wants to take care of you: *"Let's talk about hugging. We're both here for you. I want to make sure that any time we hug or do anything in here, we're taking care of you, not me. At the end of the session, if you want a hug, I'm going to ask you if you want it for you. I want you to take a moment to think about it. If 'yes,' we hug. If 'no,' we don't."*

"Boundaries and ethics protect both the client and the therapist."

- When there's always a hug at the end of the session. *"I want to check in with you about hugging. Do you ever feel like you have to when you don't really want to? Let's talk about how you know whether you want to and when you might not. It's absolutely okay not to hug the therapist!"* (Said with a smile.)
- When there's sexual attraction on either side: no hugging.
- When client doesn't want to: no hugging.
- When your licensing organization or state law prohibits it: no hugging.

Boundaries and ethics protect both the client and the therapist. They protect clients by keeping the focus on the clients; they teach clients that they have rights to their space, sovereignty, and wants; and they let clients know the rules of therapy. Boundaries and ethics protect therapists by giving us guidelines to help clients, to protect our space and time, and to keep our personal needs corralled.

7 / **Dealing with Differences**

We are social animals. We define ourselves and each other by our places in the social order. Most of us fit into a family, an ethnicity, a neighborhood, a social class, a society. Our social roles include jobs, parenting, friendships, and membership in religious and other organizations. We are defined by others, and possibly by ourselves, and by our races, ethnicities, genders, sexual identities (gender and orientation), appearances, and class markers.

We crave acceptance. In fact, acceptance in our particular milieu may be tied to our survival. When we don't fit the expectations of our families or tight social groups, we may feel shame and experience self-imposed or forced isolation. If we don't fit the societal definition of "us," we may be kept from jobs, group membership, and being treated as fully human. Or we may be harassed, assaulted, or killed for being "other." Psychotherapy must address these issues with every client.

Mark Davila (2019) says

> "On working with differences in the consulting room, we therapists should always hold that we have more power in the room than does our patient. Further, we come in to the room with

a certain set of values that may or may not be present in the culture of our patient—and in that way, have the potential of enacting a certain type of colonization. This dynamic I have found to be very rich in my work with black, brown, and Asian folks—and calling it out has always led to fruitful moments/work/patient autonomy. There is also a temptation by some to view the therapist and client relationship as somehow different or separate than the world outside the consulting room. In my work with peers, I have found that this is most often the case of a provider with white privilege working with a brown or black person, or a man working with a woman—that somehow racism and sexism has gotten checked at the door. It hasn't. With gender, male providers often miss this boat where their female patients are concerned. How is our male privilege playing out in the types of questions we ask, and in the compliance we're seeking from our female patient? This is obviously on steroids when we're working with a woman who has been traumatized by a man. Be aware that the more privilege the therapist has in the world outside, the more that needs to be held and accounted for in the consulting room—as a gravitational anchor, we need to be especially generous, and assume that negative feedback we receive from a patient is probably on target in some important way (regardless of our intention or the character structure of the patient). Further, if we receive reports from a patient about the way in which they are treated in the world (that may seem overblown to us, but are related to their station in the world), believe them. I have found this latter point to be very important around areas of racism and misogamy." (Davila, 2019, email)

To start, ASK. *"What's your relationship with your body?" "What's it like for you, being the only Black/White/Asian/Jew/immigrant/genius in the class/office/neighborhood? How do you get treated? How does that feel?" "When did you first know you were gay/trans/gender fluid/bi? When did you come out? What was that like?"* Asking opens up the sometimes-silenced topic. It shows that you're not clueless, whether you share the client's attribute or not. And it shows that you care. If the client doesn't want to talk about it, that's okay. You've left the door open.

Our differences can define our acceptability to ourselves, our families, our social milieus, and our societies. Small differences can bring shame from without and within. People who don't fit the appropriate image for their families and social milieu, by being too fat, too frail, not achieving enough, or even achieving too much, can be feel alienated and not loveable. The Two-Hand technique (Shapiro, 2005b) can help delineate the problem:

1. The client anchors "how I should be" in one hand,
2. Then anchors "how I actually am" in the other hand,
3. Then notices what emotions and thoughts arise as they hold both.

This can be modified to fit many situations:

1. "How **they** think I should be versus how I am." Skinny, top of the class, a top athlete, white, more religiously observant, etc., versus not being that way
2. "Who **they** think I am versus who I really am." They think I am stupid (because I'm female or working class or not white) but I am actually intelligent or skilled; they think I am dangerous (because I'm male, big, not white) but I am actually benign; they think I am evil/going to hell (because I'm gay, not observant, not their religion) but I am actually moral/good/connected to God.

It helps to acknowledge both the expectations and the trauma that can come from families, social groups, and society as a whole. Acknowledge bullying, shaming, missed opportunities, being treated like an idiot, and the projections that others put on the.

For black men, you may acknowledge the real dangers they face from law enforcement and ask how they deal with that. One of my clients was a black physician who moved to a small, mostly white town in Washington state. Several times in the first week he was stopped for "driving-while-Black" by sheriffs who approached the car with guns drawn. He took his family to the sheriffs' station, introduced them to the staff there, and gave several pictures of his cars and his family to the staff so that they would know not to shoot them. The police left him and his family alone after that, but the family members were still followed around any store they went into (as are many people of color all over this country) and stared at wherever they went. We acknowledged and worked on his fear for his family, his anger that his intervention was necessary, and his annoyance at the constant surveillance.

> **"When real-life dangers for someone in the threatened group make the news ask about its effect on your client."**

When real-life dangers for someone in the threatened group make the news (shootings in a synagogue or mosque, rape/harassment, police shootings), ask about its effect on your client. You might hear of terror, anger, and/or resignation. Your caring matters. And using your trauma treatment skills can be helpful. If there is trauma, once it is cleared, there may be anger and grief about past and present dangers. Normalize and support whatever the affect is. And ask your clients if there's any organization they might join for support, or even connect with online, to deal with their fears/anger/grief about the situation.

It's important to clear the past traumas of shaming, bullying, violence, and discrimination. And it's important to help your clients prepare for the future. *"How do you want to deal with the next guy who doesn't want to take 'no' for an answer?"* *"What will you do when that coworker mansplains to you again/when your mom asks about your weight/when you get passed over for the promotion because of who you are/when the next murder-by-cop happens/when the next mosque or synagogue or church shooting happens?"*

Sometimes, people can actually *do* something. Sometimes, all they can do is feel it all and think about how to take care of themselves.

(See Chapter 13, Treating Anxiety, for a case history of a woman who cleared the trauma of generations of deadly racism.)

Clearing Cultural Introjects

Identity is complicated. We can identify with and be proud of the same cultural, ethnic, or personal attributes that get us excluded, put down, or physically harmed. We can hold shame for something that others value in us. Often when there's a negative response to some of our attributes, we internalize it, and it becomes shame. Other times there's no shame, but we live with the awareness that the same cultural response will be continually projected onto us.

You can use the Two-Hand technique to work with cultural trauma:

> "Keep the 'differences' in your mind as you work with each client from any cultural context."

- *Hold the person that they think you are because you're black/working class/ blind/female/Jewish/round/queer/trans/white/smart/etc. in one hand.*
- *Hold the person that you know you are in the other hand.*
- *Sit with both of those for a moment. What do you notice now?* (If it's a negative emotion and you do EMDR, start the bilateral now!)
- *Where in your body do you hold what they think you are? What does it feel like? What's it made of? What does it look like?*
- *Do you want to keep carrying that around? No? Great. Then put on your gloves, notice the big hole that just opened in the ground next to us, pull that stuff out, and throw it down the hole. . . Keep going. . . Keep going. . . Let me know when it's all pulled out of you. Now put the lid down on that hole and flush it!*

- *What would you like inside you instead?* (Most often, my clients choose acceptance, love, healing, God's love, or "knowing that I'm okay.") *Notice the color of that and what it's made of. Now breathe it in. Fill that space completely. . . Now let it spill over the space into your whole body, filling your body completely with that acceptance/healing/ etc. Are you completely full? Then let it radiate a bit outside your body to make a shield for when the next fool treats you like someone you're not. Imagine it doing that. People are still going to be fools, but that can bounce off you now.* (Shapiro, 2005b)

Or

- *"Notice that reaction you get to your intelligence, attractiveness, kindness, accomplishment. What's your response to those responses? How do you feel when you get treated that way? How would you like to respond?"*

Keep the "differences" in your mind as you work with each client from any cultural context. And watch out for over-identification. What *you* might feel as a gay/smart/person of whatever race or class or group you are may not be the same as what your client feels. Be aware of yourself so that you can truly tune in to your clients.

8 / **Building Affect Tolerance**

People who can tolerate, accept, identify, and express their emotions are psychologically ahead of the game. They tend not to be addicts: Addicts use substances or compulsive behaviors to medicate or distract from distressing emotion. Affect tolerant people don't dissociate, because they can feel what they feel without the endogenous opioids wiping out a distressing neural pathway and replacing it with shut-down, panic, or a whole new part. Even if they're wired for anxiety, they tend not to have diagnosable anxiety disorders, since their felt and named anxiety doesn't stop them from doing what they need to do (avoidance) or eschewing what their confabulating brains tell them they must do (OCD). "That's just my anxiety talking. I'm not washing my hands for the whole next hour, even if I have a worry about contamination." They're better off in relationships, since they can accept and express what's really going on with them, even if it's embarrassing. And while they're as prone to PTSD, bipolar disorder, and psychosis as other people, they have an easier time dealing with the symptoms.

Affect tolerant people tend to have similar backgrounds. They usually started out with at least one well-attached, very responsive caregiver. This caregiver responded to positive affect (smiles and laughter) in kind, letting the smile and the smiling eye contact flow back forth, building up to even more happiness. This built up the "muscles" of positive attachment and positive feeling. When the baby was mad or sad, the caregiver responded to it with affirmation, definition and soothing: Matching the baby's tone for anger: "You're mad that I won't give you that cookie! Of course, you are! You really want it. *I'm sorry* you don't get to have it now. You can sit right here on my lap and be really mad." For sad: "Poor baby, you're so sad that I have to go work again! I'm sad too. I'll miss you and you'll miss me. You can be sad and know that I'm coming back, just like I always do." And for fear: "That was a big, loud thunderclap that scared you! It made me jump, too. And honey, you're safe here with me. It's a scary sound, but it's not going to hurt us. Let's notice the fear move out of us while we hug each other. Let's see what happens when we hear that big noise again."

So, what happened in the last paragraph? The emotion is named, explained, not shamed, and somewhat soothed. The child is taught what the emotions are, that they're normal, that they don't scare away the most important person, and that they're consolable.

The majority of psychotherapy clients did not have enough of these lovely interactions. Perhaps they expressed feelings around a preoccupied, depressed, drugged, or clueless caregiver who gave no response or gave a negative response. Since babies (and many adults) think they cause everything, they translate the lack of response to "I don't deserve a response. I'm bad." Or "I'm not doing it right. I'm ineffectual. It doesn't matter what I do." Behavior that is not reinforced often becomes extinguished. If emotion is not okay, not acknowledged, or worse, actively inhibited, kids learn shame, inhibition, and that they're not good at relationship.

There are different ways for this to come out. Parents who reinforce only positive affect, and inhibit or ignore anger, sadness, and fear, may raise children who suppress, dissociate away, and/or feel deep shame about any negative affect. These kids may develop narcissistic personalities in their efforts to hold onto their goodness and avoid the "bad," which terrifies them. Narcissists must be seen as "good"/positive by everyone around them, lest they sink into the shame-filled depression of perceived badness.

Parents who inhibit all affect but praise or just accept caregiving by their kids may raise Masterson's (1981) "closet narcissists" or codependent adults; these people try to take care of all others, not knowing nor trying to know their own needs, and they have no internal defense against shame. Their only defense is their attempt to prove their goodness by finally excelling, giving care to others, and ignoring themselves until they are seen as good enough (which they never fully take in).

Parents who actively abuse their children produce individuals with a wide range of responses that may include hypervigilance, deep shame, violently defensive reactions, or dissociation. Dissociative responses can range from spacing out during the worst of the abuse to reflexively developing different ego states for

"Behavior that is not reinforced often becomes extinguished."

each affect and experience. A horribly sexually abused child may develop a part that holds the fear of the experience, one (very pushed down) who holds the anger, one who watched from the ceiling (holding the visual experience and the chronology of the abuse), one who went away to a fantasy place during the act, one (in a dorsal vagal state) who went limp and stayed limp after it was done, and the one, more present, who holds love and affection for the abuser. These parts may pop up in stressful times, complicating the client's current life. These complications can run from becoming "frozen" when stressed to outbursts of anger to attraction to and tolerance for abusers in their current life. These kids, and the adults they become, may reflexively numb themselves or overreact to affect. If they become numb, they may not respond appropriately to current danger. If they overreact and can't self-soothe, they may become avoidant of many things: in relationships they think, "If I attach to anyone, I'll be abused"; if they feel happy, "If I feel good, then it will just be taken away.

Why bother?"; or if they have any feelings at all, "I'll just look at my phone, drink, work, and completely ignore my insides."

Affect problems and dissociation can occur without any abuse. Babies and young children who are separated from loving caregivers without any consolation can have overwhelming emotions, resulting in shutdown states that can become dissociative. If otherwise loving parents become unresponsive due to grief, illness, stress, or addiction, their kids can quickly move from trying to engage them to anger to overwhelming distress to a shut-down state. In a ZERO TO THREE film (2009), Ed Tronick shows a video that illuminates the still face experiment (see https://www.youtube.com/watch?v=apzXGEbZht0). In the video, an otherwise responsive mother lets her face go still. It takes about a minute for the baby to completely lose composure. This mother makes repair efforts a minute later, and the baby, reengaged, becomes her happy self again. Watch the video to see this response. In a longer video that Tronick shows at conferences, the mother waits a few minutes longer, and it takes much longer for the child to reengage with her and become responsive again. Now, think about children who don't experience repair for days, weeks, or longer. These kids can develop deeply entrenched neural networks of their responses to the relational cut-off, including rage states, anxiety states, and complete shutdown. Some may develop full-blown dissociative disorders, despite the lack of "abuse." For kids, inconsistent adult response, or chronic lack thereof, can be akin to abuse.

People of any age can experience overwhelming affect with a big enough trauma or loss. If they have good attachments and subsequent affect-regulation experience, they'll more easily and quickly move through the distress. Anyone can have PTSD. People with poor affect regulation are more likely to develop PTSD and will require more therapeutic intervention to clear it. They're more likely to avoid the traumatic material, to become dissociative, and to have difficulty coming back to the feeling of present safety.

Growing Affect Tolerance

Tell your clients that you're working together to rewire their brains. Clients will be moving from automatically reacting to or avoiding big feelings to being able to tolerate them and make conscious choices about how to respond. Tell them that shifting early affective wiring takes some time but is not very complicated.

Here is a way to describe the steps for working with moderate affect tolerance issues that don't involve massive dissociation:

> *"Tell your clients that you're working together to rewire their brains."*

1. *We'll work together to identify feelings and stay with them.*
2. *I'll teach you some mindfulness techniques you can do on your own.*
3. *We'll identify the triggers for the overwhelming feelings that make you switch gears and give you some things you can do instead.*
4. *We'll practice those other skills here and set you up to be able to do them on your own.*

The most important part is the therapist's presence with the client's emotion. CIMBS therapy (Sheldon & Sheldon, in press) has a wonderful way to begin this work. Sit close, make eye contact, and tell the client, *"We're here to notice and accept every thought, every emotion, and every sensation that you have."* Your clients will usually go straight into shame, "Oh, no! I'm going to be seen!" and you will say, *"What just happened? What are you noticing inside? . . . What emotion is that? . . . Where are you feeling that in your body? . . . Are there words that go with that? . . . All your emotions are welcome. Stay connected with me* and *with that feeling and stay with what happens."*

You will respond to every shift in expression or posture, every twitch, every eye blink, every change in breath with *"What do you notice now?"* bringing the client's attention to her or his own process. Every emotion is identified and welcomed the way it should have happened in childhood. You keep your connection to the client (leaning in, eyes fixed on theirs) and coach them to stay connected to you. This process starts out uncomfortable for most people, including therapists, and then becomes normal and sometimes quite joyful. When the affect becomes positive, respond eagerly, *"Notice this smile bounce back and forth between us!"* thus strengthening the neural pathways for the good stuff.

When you and your client sit with a distressing feeling, material tied to that affect will often come into the client's mind. Some memories will be perfect fodder for whatever trauma therapy you do. Some you will simply acknowledge and stay with, until the client, finally noticing the emotion and receiving a response, lets the emotion move through. Help the client notice each change as the emotion gets stronger or shifts to another. If you see the client spacing out or taking attention away from themselves, bring them back in touch with you and with her or his internal processes, *"Are you still here? Bring yourself back to your body, its sensations, and everything that's moving through you."*

Start noticing what triggers the dissociation or the shift of subject. What emotion is most likely to bring the client out of internal experience? What age goes with it? (Probably infant/toddler, sometimes older.) Start preparing the client: *"We've got anger here. See if you can stay right here with it and with us."*

No matter what other techniques you are using, respond to the shifting affect of these clients, underlining the importance of feeling and the possibility of response. Diana Fosha (2000) brings the therapist's emotions into the equation: *"What's it like for you to know that I feel very sad (angry/happy) that that happened to you?"* This ensures that clients know they're getting a response and that they consider the effect of the response throughout their brain—thoughts and feelings—while they respond to the therapist.

Attachment and affect work aren't a quick fix. It takes many weeks to install the new hardware and program it to feel, identify, tolerate, and transform difficult emotions. But you'll see constant growth. First, your clients will stop shunning the practice. Some will even look forward to it. Second, you will see their ability to stay with what they're feeling increase. People who couldn't look you in the eyes may, after a few weeks, eagerly stare into your face, free of shame and willing to be seen. Many will report how they are noticing more feelings out in the world, and are noticing who can and cannot respond to them. "I used to think it was me, but it has nothing to do with me!" People addicted to substances or behaviors that have protected them from overwhelming affect may begin to tell you that they are doing fewer drugs, or bingeing less, or not having to stay so busy.

Homework

From the very beginning, you'll give them homework:

1. Have them set an alarm to sound two to five times a day when they are to stop what they're doing, notice what they're feeling, and sit with it for five to ten minutes. Then they should write which feelings arose in a notebook or on a phone app that keeps notes.

2. And/or have them meditate for 20 minutes at least twice a day. You can teach them in your office to sit up comfortably straight, feet on the floor, and to focus on their breath moving in and then out, while noting the emotions, thoughts, and sensations that arise, and always directing their attention back to the breath. There are many free or inexpensive meditation apps that clients may find helpful. It's often easier to meditate with a guide. Some people recommend Mindfulness-Based Stress Reduction, Jon Kabat-Zinn's widely taught meditation class.

3. And have them stop when they're reaching for pot, alcohol, sugar, a game-app, porn, a betting site, or whatever else they use to avoid affect, and name the feeling or event that triggered it. If they can sit with the feeling for a few minutes, do they still want the "drug" to wipe it out?

(Sometimes they want it more!) After the break, they can write about that in their daily notes.

Check in on the homework during each session, giving praise for any movement toward consciously being with affect. Don't disparage or shame clients who can't do the homework. Instead, try to find out what's going on:

1. Is there an underlying anxiety disorder? If so, you're going to work with them to feel the anxiety without avoidance or compulsive action and teach them skills so they can notice it as a physical symptom and then calm their body down.

2. Is there a big trauma with big flashbacks any time the client isn't otherwise occupied? Use your best PTSD-eradicating technique to knock it out.

3. Is the client more dissociated than you thought, and is a "protector part" blocking emotion to protect the client from overwhelming affect, even though the affect is no longer so overwhelming? You're going to start the work of oriented parts to the present and getting their oldest-wisest self in charge.

4. Is the client resisting the nasty parent they've projected onto you? "You're not going to tell me what to do!" It's time to discuss what's happening between the two of you and get the client to notice that you and the horrid mom/dad are different people.

5. Is the client too disorganized to stop and do the work? This is when it is helpful to have them set alarms on a watch or phone for times to do it.

6. Is it just too scary for the client? Spend more time in the session sitting with the emotions. Do more mindfulness practice in sessions. Support more feeling of fear and being with it.

Affect tolerance will be an issue for many clients. You'll find that when the trauma is cleared, the body is calmer, and the neural pathways of being with emotion are strong, your clients will present differently. They will be able to identify what they feel, be present with it, and not let it run their lives. They'll report more happiness, more connection with others, and more capacity for honesty with themselves and others. Few clients come into therapy reporting, "I want to tolerate my feelings better." But most find that their ability to do just that changes their lives in many great ways.

9 / **Healing Attachment Wounds**

Attachment springs from the innate ability of babies to feel emotions and connect with their caregivers. Early attachment experiences correlate with a person's ability to regulate emotions, maintain a sense of security, connect with others, enjoy themselves, and maintain concentration.

In the 1960s and 1970s, Mary Ainsworth and colleagues (1978) did a series of studies about early attachment. In an experiment called the Strange Situation protocol, they had parents bring their toddlers into a room and leave them there alone for a while, during which time a stranger walks in, stays for three minutes, then leaves. Ainsworth noted seeking of proximity and contact; how the kids maintained contact; avoidance of proximity and contact; and resistance to contact and comforting. She also noted the exploratory and play behaviors of the kids, their search behaviors (looking at or banging on the door or the chair mom had been on), and their affect. Based on the children's behaviors while the parents were gone and when they came back, Ainsworth (1978) identified three attachment styles:

1. Secure attachment: These kids smile when their parents return,

they rush to their parent to be soothed, and after a while, they calm down and look for something to do. Securely attached kids expect care, expect to be soothed, are most likely to explore their environment, and are generally the happiest and healthiest kids. As adults these people can love, tolerate affect, and connect without clinging. About 70% of the kids in the study demonstrated secure attachment.

2. Anxious–ambivalent attachment: These kids are highly distressed, they don't explore much while their parent is gone, and they are wary of strangers. On their parent's return, these kids may be quite angry or very passive, approaching the parent, but resisting contact.

> **"Attachment springs from the innate ability of babies to feel emotions and connect with their caregivers."**

Ainsworth says that these kids don't expect their caregivers to take care of them and are wary of them when they return. These kids cry more and explore less than securely attached kids. As adults, they may exhibit borderline personality, jumping from anxiously grabbing for attachment to either rage or collapse when their needs aren't getting met. They may hang on too tightly to abusive or unsuitable partners. Or they may become chronically codependent, taking care of everyone around them, without paying attention to their own needs.

3. Avoidant attachment: While their parent is out of the room, these kids do not look upset, though their bodies show acute distress. They don't show fear of a stranger being around. When the parent returns, the child may not even look up (though his or her brain imaging shows that with the return of the parent, the child is much calmer.) These kids don't differentiate much between their parents and strangers. Ainsworth says that these kids are likely to have a caregiver who is insensitive or rejecting of their needs, and who may be unavailable during times of emotional distress. Avoidant kids don't expect care and try to appear unmoved by proximity to their parents. They may grow up to be loners, avoiders of intimacy, and often struggle with depression.

Later, Bowlby (1988) added disorganized attachment to the list: "Disorganized" kids have scary parents, who either abuse them or respond weirdly or unpredictably. These kids want to flee, but the person they want to flee to for protection is also the person who scares them. They have no control and no good strategy for achieving safety or calming their distress. Often, the only way they have to deal with such an overwhelming situation is dissociation. As kids, they exhibit odd or ambivalent behavior toward their parent: approaching the parent for comfort, then backing off or becoming combative or even assaultive. As adults they have trouble forming a coherent narrative, which is one of the signs of dissociation, according to Mary Main and colleagues (2008). They are likely to crave relationships yet be unable to maintain them. If in a relationship, they can go from attempting to connect to either shutting down or exploding when the relationship becomes too close. Many abusers were kids with disorganized attachments. Many victims of domestic violence get stuck in relationships with their abusers, dissociating when the abuse starts and being unable to leave, just like at their original home.

When you do intakes, watch for attachment styles.

1. Is your client able to look you in the eyes, speak coherently about their childhood, appropriately express emotion, and report that they had good, consistent parenting?
2. Are they anxiously scanning your face to see if you approve, if they're okay, and that you're not going to explode at them?
3. Do they become belligerent, especially when the therapeutic relationship becomes close?
4. When you ask, *"When you were little, what was your life like with your parents?"* does their narrative fall apart, "Um, it was okay . . . I guess. Um, my mom, um, was nice . . . Well, sometimes . . ."
   Or do they shift from one narrative, to another: Angry, then shut down? Coherent, then mumbling? (Main, 1991)
5. Pay special attention to how your clients relate to you. Watch for

this while you're asking the other questions. What kind of a person do they treat you as: Scary? A savior? A monster? Someone who doesn't really care? Or do their projections alternate? Sometimes you're the savior, sometimes the devil, though you haven't shifted your behavior.

During your intake session, notice the client's relationship history:

1. Are they in a stable, supportive relationship, with lots of friends, and are they firmly entrenched in a good community?
2. Have they been in one rotten, abusive relationship after another?
3. Do they have no friends? Or no nonexploitive friends?
4. Are they avoidant of intimacy with everyone?
5. Are they taking care of everyone around them, with no expectation of reciprocity?

Repairing Dysfunctional Attachment

Your job is to be a wonderful attachment object: safe, responsive, delighted in the presence of your client, consistent, connected, and attuned, with appropriate boundaries.

1. You greet clients warmly when asking them in.
2. You sit closely, no more than a few feet away. For clients who were sexually or physically abused by someone of your gender, you may need to speak about safety and boundaries: *"We're sitting closely in order to wake up the attachment circuits in your brain. If that feels uncomfortable, let's talk about it. I want you to know that I will stay right here, and I will be keeping my hands off of you."* And for clients who become sexually attracted to you as you sit so closely, *"All your emotions are welcome. What's it like to have those feelings here with me, knowing that we will never act on them? What other emo-*

tions are you having along with those sexual ones? Notice how those feelings transform as we sit with them."

3. You maintain eye contact, most of the time. (And you'll develop the capacity to maintain eye contact and attunement, without a break, for the entire session.)

4. You respond to changes in affect, stance, subject, and "energy" in the client with

   a. *"What just happened?"*

   b. *"I notice a shift."*

   c. Or make an adjustment in your own stance to mirror theirs.

5. If the client is trying to please you, push you away, seduce you, take care of you, or avoid being seen, you bring it up kindly and with curiosity: *"What's happening inside you when you turn away?"* Or, *"You're saying some pretty sexual things to me. Is there something you're avoiding while you're doing that?"* Or, *"I'm noticing how you're taking care of me, right now. First, you need to know that I'm going to care for you and be here for you, even if you don't. Second, I'm supposed to be taking care of you. What's going on inside, when you're taking care of me?"* Or, *"I'm noticing a feeling coming through you. All your emotions are welcome here. Can you let me know what's coming up?"*

   > **"Know that attachment issues can take a while to heal."**

6. Whatever comes up for your clients is grist for the therapeutic mill. Often times, clients will go into grief for what didn't happen the first time around. Let them feel it. Sometimes that grief turns into anger. Welcome it. Sometimes the anger will be at you for not being available 24/7 or for a different kind of relationship. Hang with it, it's progress that they can communicate that anger and have it be received. (Just remember, that it may be *at* you, but it's not *about* you.) Sometimes the old hopelessness arises. Welcome the feeling, but contain it: *"You and I can sit with this old feeling together. Notice what happens when we give you loving attention*

as you feel that old hopelessness." And for clients with avoidant or ambivalent attachment, who are pushing you away, *"Feel that old fear and protectiveness. Let's hold them together, in this present, safe room. Notice how they are trying to protect you from more disappointment. And notice how they keep you away from here-and-now connections, while attempting to protect . . . So just look, and feel, and accept that feeling, while connecting right here with me, and notice what happens."*

Know that attachment issues can take a while to heal. If someone had poor nurturance as a child and few good "attachment objects" as an adult, they may not have the wiring for connection, for feeling safe, or for calming down. In attachment therapy, you're rewiring the person to be able to accept caring, to connect inside with emotions, and to feel safe doing so. When your clients tell you that therapy is taking too long, you need to remind them that it took years to put in the old programs and hardware and that the two of you are changing hardware and software, which takes a while.

Ego State Work with Attachment Issues

Ego state therapy is widely used with attachment issues. Connecting the distressed child part of the client to his or her functional and nurturing adult part allows for good healing experiences. Here's are some examples:

1. *Take a moment to notice the most adult parts of you: that brilliant software designer and that great mom. Think of a time when you were doing a good job with those kids of yours and tell me about it . . . Good! We're going to use that good mom for the healing of some younger parts of you.*

2. *Bring that good mom/dad/engineer/responsible guy that you are back in time to the day you were born, to the hospital you were born in. Go to*

that big window that has the newborn babies behind it and point out the one with your name on it. The nurse picks up the baby and directs you to a little room with a comfortable rocking chair, and hands you the swaddled baby. Look in that baby's eyes, and notice how they peer back at you. Feel that baby's weight in your arms while they feel your strong arms holding them. Notice that baby responding to your voice as you respond to every sound and cry they make. Tell them 'I'm so glad you're here!' and watch them wriggle in delight. Look this baby over and notice that they're perfect and make sure you tell them that. Then tell that baby, 'I'm here for you every moment. My job is to respond to your needs, and to take delight in you. If you're sad, I'm here. If you're happy and playful, I'm here. If you're mad, I'm here. And I'm going to make sure you eat well, get lots of sleep, feel lots of love, and are connected, through me, to love and joy in the world.' Feel your love moving to and through that baby, and feel the connection coming back through them. I'm going to give you one of April Steele's (2007a) Imaginal Nurturing CDs or MP3s to listen to every day for two weeks, which will walk you through this exercise, to let you build even more connection and nurturing with that kid inside! (Steele, 2007b).

3. In Lifespan Integration (Pace, 2007), the adult goes back to their birth or a traumatic or neglected time. There, the adult picks up the child, comforts it, and brings it up through the years, one at a time, to the present time. Then the adult orients the child to the present and promises to protect and take care of it. The adult goes back and brings the child to the present several times, until the client can't find any of that child or its affect in the past.

4. When babies don't receive responses or they receive an abusive response, they learn that some or all of their emotions aren't important. They may shut their emotions down and/or develop responses that might, if loud enough or specific enough, get a caregiver's attention. These responses, or lack thereof, become neural highways of behavior that we call personality disorders.

    a. In people with borderline personality disorder (BPD), you may find a normal-appearing functional part, a clingy "baby" part that can't stand being alone (or the end of the session, or the therapist leaving town), a part that completely idolizes you (or anyone who meets their needs), and an angry part that sees you as totally evil. The ultimate therapeutic goals are to get the mindful, functional part to run the show and to heal and integrate the affective/younger/automatic states. You do this by showing up lovingly for all parts, repeatedly calling out the oldest, wisest, most functional part to help take care of the idealizing kid and the angry/defender, and doing all the trauma work and attachment-based therapies that each part needs until all are healed. (I've written more extensively about this in *Easy Ego State Interventions,* Shapiro, 2016.)

b. Clients with narcissist personality disorder (NPD) are run by shame. Their "adult" part is busy defending the younger shame-filled part. They need to brag, look perfect, and never need correction. They "know" that if anyone disagrees with them or sees them as less than perfect, their cover of goodness is blown and they are the completely worthless person that they feel like underneath. Some narcissists are too busy charming you to feel their shame. Some are too busy attacking your competence to feel their shame. Either way, you will be doing the early attachment and trauma work with their "worthless" child parts, and at the same time building the client's capacity to feel the old shame, until the client knows that they're okay and that there's no need for the defense.

5. When I'm working with highly dissociated clients with very disrupted or disruptive younger parts or with a client who has a phobia of younger parts of themself, I do this: *Since this child part needs lots of care, we're getting it a full-time caregiver. Who would be the most nurturing and healing being you know that could take care of this child? This person may be a clone of someone, or a great TV or movie mother or father, or (Since*

you're having trouble imagining someone, and I know you have religion) how about an angel? Unlike human parents, the nurturer you choose never has to sleep, eat, or go to the bathroom. Let's put this angel in a wonderful healing room with everything a child could ever need: food, toys, a nice crib/bed, and a great chair for holding that little you. I want you to hand this child to this angel in this healing room. Every moment that you are awake, asleep, or doing anything in the outside world, that child is being held and responded to. Every need is met. Every emotion has a healing response. Everything about this child is welcomed. And we're going to speed up time in that healing place. Every minute in your outside world is an hour in that inside room, so by next week, when we meet again, that baby will have been held, and fed, and responded to for many months. You can check in once a day to see how that baby and its caregiver are doing.

"As clients grow the neural pathways of better attachment, they become more tolerant of their emotions, more connected to others."

a. On occasion, some clients with borderline personality disorder or DID might insist that you are the only one that can be in that inside room. One way to handle that is to say, *"I can't do it, but my clone can. My clone is different from me, in that she has no other clients and no outside life and no human needs. She will have perfect attention around the clock, and unlike me, she never makes mistakes, and she always knows the most nurturing thing to do. In fact, unlike me, she can intuit every need that that child has. Just don't get us confused!"*

In these examples, the therapist is shifting the client's brain by creating experiences that they may have never had, or that they need to have more of. If the clients record the caregiving instructions on their smartphones, they can listen to them daily and recreate the experience, building more experiences of attachment and care. When the clients are more attached inside, you can begin to help them navigate outside relationships more adeptly. Use their adult parts to remind their kid parts that they no longer have to put up with abuse to be loved. Remind the adult parts that they get to pick good adult partners. And in negotiating with those partners, their adult parts get to decide how to set boundaries, to argue, and to compromise.

As clients grow the neural pathways of better attachment, they become more tolerant of their emotions, more connected to others, and more capable of choosing safe, attachable friends and partners. You will be able to notice and celebrate these shifts as therapy continues.

10 / **Building Skills**

People who don't need therapy had families and social milieus that taught them the necessary tools to get along in life. They may have watched their parents do things and been coached to plan, begin, work through, and complete tasks. They have experienced loving connections and know how to make "bids" for or repair breaches in those connections. And they have been supported to feel, express, and move through affect. These people were supported to know and express what they want and don't want, and to handle the disappointment of not always getting it. And they know how to amuse themselves, without developing an addiction to avoiding everything else. Many clients don't have those skills and need to experience, and practice, them in therapy. The practice is important. "Knowing" about a skill doesn't "set" it into accessible neural pathways the way "doing" it can. As much as you can, give experiences, not lectures.

Therapists have to be careful with this. We don't want to lose the attachment-and-transformation part of our roles to advice-giving. All skill-building must take place in the context of therapeutic support, awareness of the client's history and self, and the goals of transformation. Yet, new behaviors can be transforming. The first time an over-pleasing client says an emphatic "No!" can be life-changing. So can an equally emphatic "I want this!" Let these be causes for celebration in your sessions.

Self-Care

Some people may not have learned the basics of good diet, exercise, and sleep hygiene. Sometimes, you, the therapist, are the only person who knows and is in a position to give basic advice about it. You can give advice and turn people on to resources that speak to their issues. You can help people set up schedules for sleep, exercise, and eating. On occasion, this will be the most life-changing intervention that you do.

- Sleep is essential. If your client isn't sleeping find out why. Are they on social media until 2 a.m.? Are they avoiding PTSD-induced nightmares? Are they out at the bar? Talk them into going to bed. Explain that sleep has a strong impact on all aspects of health, and especially mood. Have them try shutting down all screens an hour before a reasonable bedtime. And ask them about sleep every week. Have them try to sleep for eight hours each night for a week, and report back. They may be amazed by the results.
- The typical American diet is high in carbohydrates and low in the protein and vegetables that we all need. Have your clients do some research on what healthy eating habits are and find a way to get good food that's not too onerous. Suggest that they eat three good meals and a nutritious snack each day. One trick: if people are eating a lot of good food, they're not going to be hungry for too much sugar or carbs. Another trick: get them to feed other people. They're going to want to take good care of their friends and may be motivated to cook better stuff for others. Let clients know that nutritious microwave meals are possible. So is switching from burger-and-fries to good Chinese takeout.
- Exercise is essential, especially for anxious or depressed clients. It can also be a way for isolated clients to connect with others. There might

be a running or hiking group, a yoga or aerobics class, or a supportive weight-lifting coach in your isolated client's future. And even if the walk, run, or workout is solo, the rise in energy, affect, and mindfulness is helpful for nearly every person.

- Bodywork, haircuts, or spa days can be assigned to people who can afford them. Even a $10 haircut can help someone feel cared for. It's not your job to comment on your client's appearance. But it is your job to assist them in figuring out what would help them feel nurtured and how to put it into practice.

Finding and Expressing Affect

Some people come from families, cultures, or situations that didn't support the expression of feelings. These people may not know what they're feeling or feel uncomfortable expressing what they do feel. For some of these clients, the body is a bad neighborhood where the feelings live and that should be avoided at all costs. Without access to our feelings, it's often hard to know what we want and don't want, to make decisions, to show empathy (or have it), and to express needs. Here are some ways to introduce clients to that neighborhood and to the skills that come from body awareness:

1. **For awareness**: *"Take a deep breath. Feel your breath move all the way to your belly. Raise your shoulders. Now drop them. Now notice the other sensations in your body. Where are you holding tension? What's relaxed? Notice your breath; is it flowing easily, or is there some holding or tightness in your chest . . . Now think about something or someone you love. What happens in your body when you do that? What do you notice? . . . Think about something that scares you. Where does that live? . . . Now something that makes you angry. Where's that? What sensation goes with that?"*
2. **For making choices**: *"Which do you like better, chocolate or vanilla?*

Where do you notice chocolate in your body? What sensation goes with that? Where's vanilla? What does that feel like?" Continue this line with *"Steak or tofu? Boys or girls? Democrats or Republicans? Sunny days or clouds? Superhero movies or romantic comedies?"* and other choices. Give them some time after each pair of choices to notice their sensations. If they need more tools for a particular choice, introduce them to the Two-Hand Technique (Shapiro, 2005b): *"In one hand hold taking the new job. In the other, hold staying in the old one. What do you notice when you focus on your right hand? . . . On your left? What do you feel in your body? What emotion goes with that?"*

> **"Without access to our feelings, it's often hard to know what we want and don't want."**

3. **"I want!"** *"I'm going to ask you what you want, over and over. Notice what it is you want and where you feel it, and tell me, emphatically, what it is. What do you want?*" "World Peace!" *"Where do you feel that in you? Tell me you want it."* "I want peace." *"Louder!"* "I WANT PEACE!" *"Good job! And what do you want now?"* "Lunch!" *"What do you want to eat?"* "Pizza!" *"Where do you feel that hunger for pizza?"* "On my tongue and in my stomach." *"Tell me you want pizza!"* etc. Go through at least five things, "training" your client to notice the wants and say them out loud. This works especially well with codependent caregivers who take care of everyone else and neglect themselves.

4. **Saying "No!"** This one is very fun. Tell your client to say a firm, loud "No!" regardless of what you say, and notice what it feels like to do so. With your tone, go from wheedling to whining to angry/manipulative: *"Please? . . . Oh c'mon, just do it! . . . I really want you to . . . Don't be a bitch/bastard! . . . Don't you care about me? . . . Just do it!"* The client gets to experience the pull to agree and to practice not caving in. Practice lays down some neural tracks that grow new, unforgettable behaviors. To make this exercise even more powerful (for your most namby-pamby, too-passive clients), have the client do it in the standing-up-straight, chin-and-chest-thrust-out, hands-on-hips "Power Pose" (Cuddy, 2012).

Containing and Calming Affect

Mindfulness

Mindfulness—the ability to identify, tolerate, and calm emotions, bodily reactions, and thoughts—is a wonderful part of or adjunct to every therapy. Here is a generic mindfulness exercise with embedded ideas for motivating your clients to do it. This exercise especially helpful for anxious, reactive, or dissociative clients.

Close your eyes. Bring your attention to your breath. Notice it coming into your nose and your lungs. Notice that moment when the inhale turns into an exhale, and notice the air moving out. Then notice when it turns to an inhale again and keep noticing the sensations of the air moving in and out of your body. Pause.

As you breathe, emotions, sensations, and thoughts will arise. Name them, "That's anxiety"; "That's a thought"; "That's a pain." Then pull your attention back to your breath. Keep noticing, and keep refocusing to the breath. Notice each thought and feeling that floats by in the stream of your awareness. The more you do this, the stronger your focus will become. Pause.

Bring your attention back to your breath. Breathe in, noticing when the exhale comes, breathe out, noticing the inhale coming. That's right. I'll let you be with this for the next five minutes . . .

Bring yourself back to this room. What do you notice now? . . . I'd like you to practice this at least once a day for ten minutes and work up to twenty minutes a day. What time of day would be best for you? Would you like to put an alert on your watch or phone to remind you? Do that right now. There are many phone apps for meditation. You can try a few. Some are for specific issues, such as anxiety or anger. You might want to check them out. The more you do this, the more you'll be able to notice when you go into an anxious, angry, or dissociative state and to bring yourself to the present safety/balance. There's a great meditation class at _____. It's a good way to get support for learning how to do this.

Emotion Calming

Both mindfulness and the many techniques discussed in Chapter 13, Treating Anxiety, can be helpful for calming other emotions. Here are two techniques that can be helpful whether the emotions come from recent trauma, a restimulated angry, clingy, defensive, or avoidant personality-disordered state, or the fight that a couple is having in your office. Most emotions are welcome in session. Use these when the client is feeling out of control and unable to just *be* with a feeling.

> **Gravity & Grounding:** *Notice gravity holding you in your chair. Lift different body parts and drop them. Imagine a cord or a root that runs into the ground from the bottom of your spine and from each foot, rooting you like a tree. Imagine breathing down the cords into the ground.*

> **Silencing the Alarm:** *Feel where the emotion is in your body. Put the heel of your right hand on your left eyebrow, near the nose. Brush your hand from your nose to behind your ear and down your neck to the point of your shoulder. Flatten your hand and brush from your shoulder to the point of your elbow and off the back of your hand. Do this three times, then do the exercise three times on the other side of the body. Keep doing complete sets until the emotion eases.*

Rehearsing Assertiveness

Many women, abuse and neglect survivors, as well as certain ethnic and cultural groups have been taught to please everyone, to not ask for anything for themselves, and to never say no. When you've done enough trauma and attachment work and practiced the "I want" and "No!" exercises with these clients, it's time to consider real-life situations and walk them through what they can say and how they want to act. It's helpful to give guidelines: *"Passive behavior is agreeing, no matter what. Aggressive communication is attacking, critical, and unwilling to compromise. Assertive communication is connecting and listening to the other person and standing up for what you want. In this situation with that person, what do you want for yourself? How do you want to tell that person what you want them to hear? Let's rehearse a few situations, starting with a situation in which they disagree with you and you need to convince them of something. Then we'll practice a situation in which they do agree with you . . . Okay. Sit up in your chair. Look me in the eyes. And start the conversation, stating clearly what it is about. I'll be a jerk the first time."*

Then proceed to play the part of the other person, acting the way your client expects that person to behave. (This can be quite fun for both of you.) You can coach the client on the side, using a different tone, if need be. And don't forget to applaud your client for stating their wants clearly and for standing their ground.

You can rehearse any number of situations, including break-ups, setting limits with children, resolving work issues, asking for raises, and telling harassers to back off. I have helped clients rehearse doing "side hugs" instead of full-frontal hugs, sharing diagnoses, dealing with street harassment, turning people down, wedding proposals, saying no, and saying YES!

Thought Switching

Every therapy has a cognitive component. Cognitive behavior therapy (CBT) has given us "thought stopping," the practice of watching your mind go down a dysfunctional path (obsession, rumination, bad choices, regret, etc.) and redirecting it. It's especially useful with people who struggle with obsessive–compulsive disorder (OCD). Here's an example:

Jim was an electrician with OCD. He worked in new construction. Several times He noticed that after installing wiring and watching drywallers enclose the work he did, he began to obsess that there might be a problem with the wiring, and requested that they tear it down so that he could check it, which lost him several jobs. I taught him to throw up his hand and say "Stop it!" every time these thoughts came to his head and to then use some calm down exercises. On the job, he changed "Stop it!" to "F—k it!" which was more powerful for him, and he stopped losing work.

Gratitude Practices

According to many researchers, including Wong and Brown (2017), gratitude practice makes measurable changes in the brain, mood, and behavior of its practitioners.

"Gratitude practice makes measurable changes in the brain, mood, and behavior."

1. "Thank you" is the simplest. Try it yourself. Notice your in breath, and say "Thank you" for breathing. Think about the people who love you: "Thank you." The bed you sleep in and the roof over it: "Thank you." The school you go to or the work you do: "Thank you." Whatever beauty you behold, fun you have, connections you make, food you eat, art you connect with: "Thank you." Some of us do this before rising in the morning and start the day in gratitude. It works.
2. Written gratitude lists are especially helpful for clients who procrastinate. Have your depressed client write a list of three things they're grateful for and bring it to their session.
3. Gratitude letters are also helpful. Clients can write letters to people they're grateful to, explaining what they are grateful for and why.

4. Religious clients can thank whatever form of God they pray to every day for the gifts they've received.

5. Trauma survivors can also say, "And thank you that I'm not in that household/battleground/horrible marriage/etc." to help themselves know that they are free of that episode.

Other Skills

Practicing Active, Reflective Listening

This training is most often needed by men, anxious people, narcissists, and people on the autism spectrum. Make sure you get them to talk about the emotions they perceive in the other person. And give them the language to express those perceptions. Have them tell you something, then reflect what you heard and perceived back to them. Then have them listen to your story and reflect back what they heard and perceived to you. For people who didn't learn these skills in their families, the Center for Nonviolent Communication offers classes and books that teach wonderful communication skills (Rosenberg, 2012).

"Putting Yourself in the Equation"

Some clients learned to take care of everyone else, to their own detriment. Teach them the Platinum Rule: "Fill your own cup first. Give away only what's left over." Then walk them through several people and situations with which they will need to put this rule into practice.

Cultural Education

For people who are from a different culture, you may tip them off to some cultural cues of the one they're learning to navigate.

Dialectical Behavior Therapy

This is a training program, started for people with borderline personality disorder, that teaches mindfulness and cognitive behavior therapy (CBT) skills and that can be useful for treating addicts, anxiety disorders, and overwhelming affect.

Resources

You can refer your clients to specific websites for all kinds of information, if they are so inclined, and save your therapy sessions for more transformational work. You may know of skill-building or mindfulness/meditation classes in your area for clients that need more here-and-now focus, who are fighting dissociation, and who live in anxious bodies.

11 / **Treating Trauma**

The American Psychiatric Association's (2013) definition of post-traumatic stress disorder (PTSD) tells us that PTSD arises after "a life-threatening event" that triggers "intense fear, helplessness, or horror." It goes on to say that such events may include rape, war, car accidents, or cataclysmic events. People with PTSD suffer intrusive dreams or visual, cognitive, or physical flashbacks of the event with a sense that it is still happening in the present. They try to avoid anything that reminds them of the trauma. When they are reminded, they may have huge physical and emotional reactions. They may feel dissociative symptoms: numbness, hyperarousal, hopelessness, estrangement, or a sense of not being themselves. They may be sleepless and angry and find it hard to focus. And they may feel that they or the world are doomed. When symptoms are present within a month of the bad event, they are considered to be acute stress disorder. After a month, the continuing presence of these symptoms is considered PTSD.

In my own and many other therapists' clinical experience, it doesn't take a life-threatening event to create a trauma reaction. Babies display the biological markers of trauma if their mothers show a still, nonresponsive face for a minute or two (Tronick, 2009). Children or adults may show a trauma response to an angry, yelling parent, boss, or partner; a job loss or other occupational stress; panic attacks and other body-generated states; or an embarrassing situation. Successful therapy can heal these relational traumas with positive changes in affect, behavior, and cognition.

Stephen Porges (2017) has an elegant explanation of what trauma does to us. He describes how the vagal nerve runs through the torso up to the brain and has three parts. The ventral vagal is the front part of the nerve, the dorsal is the back, and

"It doesn't take a life-threatening event to create a trauma reaction."

the unmyelinated is the part of the nerve that does not have a myelin sheath, which is associated with more minute and voluntary muscle control, such as facial expressions. When the myelinated ventral vagus is engaged, we can eat, connect with other people, and use our big brains to work, create, and be interested in what's around us. When we sense a threat, the unmyelinated ventral vagus puts us into a mobilized state, capable of scanning for danger and defending ourselves. We cannot eat normally, connect socially, or use much intellectual capacity when we're mobilized. When we think we're going to be killed, or after a long-extended mobilized state, the dorsal vagus becomes active, turning down every function except those necessary for baseline physical survival—breathing and heart function—which is an immobilized state. When we're not being threatened, these three functions of the vagal system constantly and subtly adjust our bodies, including our brains. Momentary, not-too-big but distressing experiences can mobilize the system then fade away as the system adjusts. Stronger, longer, developmentally ill-timed, or repetitive trauma can have long-lasting effects.

Complex Traumatic Stress Disorders

Chronic exposure to childhood abuse or neglect can reshape personalities around the pathology of trauma. Researchers and clinicians are developing new diagnoses for these complex traumatic stress disorders. Developmental trauma disorder (DTD) is a diagnosis for children who have the following:

> A. Chronic exposure to interpersonal trauma, including abandonment, betrayal, or witnessing or receiving any form of abuse.
> B. A triggered pattern of repeated emotional, somatic, behavioral, relational, self-blaming or cognitive dysregulation in response to trauma cues.
> C. Persistently altered attributions and expectancies, including distrust, negative self-attribution, lack of recourse or belief in help or justice, and a sense of inevitability of future victimization.
> D. Functional impairment in educational, peer, legal, or vocational spheres (van der Kolk, 2005).

These children are often dissociative, too passive, or too unruly and are likely to be misdiagnosed with ADHD or be insufficiently diagnosed with depression.

Kids with DTD can turn into adults with disorders of extreme stress not otherwise specified (DESNOS; Luxenberg, Spinazzola, & van der Kolk, 2001). DESNOS clients have trouble regulating their emotions. They may be angry, suicidal, and either obsequious or engaging in risky or self-destructive behaviors. They may be dissociative, with amnesia for traumatic events. And they may feel ineffective, damaged for life, over-responsible for their problems, and consequently full of shame. Relationally, they may find it hard to trust anyone, find it hard to believe that anyone can understand them, and be prone to revictimization (if you can't trust anyone, you don't know what trustworthy looks like). They can be untrustworthy themselves, from being unable to keep commitments to being downright violent. Many have somatic symptoms: stomachaches, chronic pain, asthma, heart palpitations, dissociative conversion symptoms (e.g., numb body parts or hysterical blindness), or pain in their reproductive organs or the body part that was hurt when they were abused. They may feel that either they are hopeless or the world is. They may have little tolerance for or ability to feel happiness. The following vignettes describe first the development of DID and then the development of DESNOS.

Developmental Trauma Disorder

You were bad. If you weren't, your mom would have looked you in the eyes. She'd have picked you up when you cried, and played the peek-a-boo game with you. At first, when she didn't respond, you'd try hard to get her attention, first being your cutest, then screaming. Nothing worked. You went dorsal, spacing out. It turned out that spacing out was a useful trick. When your dad starting doing sex on you, first you'd get mobilized: scared, waiting, waiting, waiting for the pain. Then you'd space out again. It worked pretty well. It even worked for the beatings, after they got going. After he was done, you felt like a dishrag, unable to move. During their fights, you'd start out tense, fearful, then sink back into that daze, if they didn't focus on you. As you grew up, you learned to cope. You went to school, played, studied. You were like a different person when you were out of the house. But sometimes the inside life intruded on your outside life. You couldn't have close friends because everyone seemed scary. You couldn't say no to anyone about anything, because you couldn't say no at home. And anyway, you were supposed to rely on yourself, nobody else. Once in a while, all the rage would come out on somebody, usually someone you cared about. They'd do something little and you'd blow, saying terrible things. For a while, they would look to you like they were totally evil. Later, they wouldn't seem so awful to you, and you'd feel totally ashamed about how you were to them.

Sometimes you felt numb. Sometimes the smallest things could bring up huge anger or fear, for no good reason. Sometimes it felt like there was a huge hole in your stomach that could never get filled. It helped to eat and eat and eat. Sometimes, when the feelings were too big or the numbness too pervasive, you'd yank on your hair, or smash your fist on your leg. It was strange that hurting made you feel better. If it was really bad, sometimes you used a knife.

The headaches started when you were little. They were constant. Sometimes your ears would buzz, too. And most of the time, if you paid attention to it, your stomach hurt. It made it hard to study or even pay attention. Feeling too much or not feeling anything were like screens between you and the world.

There was nothing to do about it. The abuse is what you were for. You were there to not get in Mom's way, and to help Dad by taking all his rage and sex. And you always failed. Mom was still depressed. Dad was still angry. You failed at the only things you were there to do. If you had been a good person, it would have been different. But you were born a failure.

People say now, "Why didn't you do anything?" Like go to the cops. Why? What's the use? The parents would deny everything. Nothing would happen. And who would believe you? Even if they did, who else would have wanted you? (Shapiro, 2010, pp. 7–8)

Disorders of Extreme Stress Not Otherwise Specified

You grew up and got madder. Mad at other people; mad at yourself. Sometimes you're mad enough or hopeless enough to try to kill yourself, and that's become one more thing that you've tried and failed. Since you got away from the parents, you cry more. When you cry, it's really scary and out of control. Sometimes when the feelings start, it's like you're not you. You're just watching yourself cry from somewhere else. It's like when you used to float up to the ceiling when he was having sex on you.

You've connected with some other people, the wrong people, of course. There must be a sign on your back, "Only dates assholes." It's so intense and wonderful in the beginning, before it goes bad. And when it goes bad, you still need them. When they're not beating you up, you can hurt yourself. You know how to cut just deep enough for maximum effect. You've got scars upon scars upon scars. It might be the only thing you're good at. When you get your tattoos, it's like getting someone else to do it for you.

You don't think much about when you were at home. In fact, if people ask, you can barely remember what it was like. If you try to talk about it, the words don't come out very well. The therapist says, "Incoherent narrative" and "dissociation". Whatever that means. Sometimes, you'll totally switch. You'll get so mad, or so scared, for no good reason, that it doesn't feel like you. And there's no way to put on the brakes. You just leave, either by spacing out or by yelling and walking out. Failing again.

Even though you're trying the therapy thing, you know it won't work. Nothing will. You're such a loser that you haven't been able to keep a job, a relationship, or even a friendship.

> Who would want you? And nobody understands you. Who could? And what's the point, really? You can't even do the simple things that the therapist asks for: "Stay with that feeling." "Tell me what it is." "Tell me what happened." Nothing. Loser.
>
> The headaches and the ear buzzing have gotten worse, especially when you try to think about the past. It hurts "down there" a lot of the time. And speaking of "down there," whenever you try to "do it," you end up thinking it's your father. That's just sick.
>
> It won't get better. And you're running out of options. Life sucks. It's hopeless. You're hopeless." (Shapiro, 2010, 11–14)

All of these disorders are treatable. With the right therapies, especially EMDR or somatic therapies, you might find that simple PTSD, such as from a car accident or a dog bite, can be cleared in a few sessions. It will take much longer to clear the symptoms of complex trauma from a whole childhood, a war, or a long, violent relationship, but they can be impacted or cleared with appropriate therapy.

Van der Hart's Theory of Structural Dissociation (van der Hart, Nijenhuis, & Steele, 2006) is a great lens through which to understand traumatized clients. Primary structural dissociation is simple PTSD, in which a generally functional, nondissociated person experiences a traumatic event and splits into two consciousness: the nontraumatized "apparently normal person" (ANP), who functions normally and is completely oriented to the present and the "emotional part" (EP), which holds the flashbacks, bad dreams, startle response, and other trauma symptoms and feels as if they're back in the trauma. The ANP tries to avoid anything that brings up the EP, which is why many clients don't want to focus on the traumas that brought them to therapy. I believe EPs develop to protect us from danger. Something hurt or frightened us, and our amygdalae and hippocampi keep saying, "Watch out! Or it might happen again!"

Secondary structural dissociation arises when there have been repetitive, usually early, attachment breaches or other repeated trauma. The ANP is the normal, social, functional part. There are usually two or more EPs with different deeply engrained functions. The EPs of secondary structural dissociations hold the parts that we see in people with personality disorders. For instance, a person with borderline personality disorder (BPD) might have a very functional ANP that lives in what Porges (2017) called a "socially connected" state, but when triggered may mobilize an EP that is ultrasensitive to abandonment, is overdependent in every relationship, cries easily, pleads for you to extend the session, and acts like a little kid. Another mobilized EP may see you or other people as evil or dangerous and as someone they should shun or attack. And they may have an immobilized EP that is completely and passively depressed. BPD clients may flip between one and the other state, making them challenging for many therapists to work with.

A person with narcissistic personality disorder (NPD) will have at their core an immobilized, shame-filled, passive, hopeless EP. This EP is protected and denied by their ANP, which holds an inflated sense of self. They will also have a mobilized EP that may attack anything and anyone that begins to trigger that sense of badness. A simple disagreement can bring out the mobilized EP, ready to attack. The unconscious defense runs like this: "At heart, I know I'm completely worthless. I can't stand feeling that, so I'm going to pretend that everything about me is great. If anyone disagrees with me or complains about anything I do, it means that I truly am that horrible worthless jerk. So, I need to fight them on that and focus on being good and in control." Therapists need to work around this defense to heal the shame-filled wound in these clients.

In tertiary structural dissociation, which includes dissociative identity disorder, there are at least two ANPs and several EPs. There is amnesia between many parts. The parts may have different roles in the system, different ages, and different names. These EPs may feel as if and believe that they live in the distressing past. The ANPs will often "lose time," not remember what happened, when the EPs are present and out front. And ANPs often have a phobia of knowing about or connecting with EPs.

Simple Trauma: Primary Structural Dissociation

Recent single traumas are the easiest to go after. They may include a car accident with no fatalities, a single rape, a dog-bite, being fired, or some other distressing event. If the client is otherwise functional, oriented to the present, and not dissociative (except for the current PTSD symptoms), you can work directly with them, to clear out the trauma.

Therapeutic interventions for these clients should include focus on and awareness of the somatic, cognitive, and emotional symptoms, with some sort of method that promotes a dual attention that keeps the client in the here and now while they sit with the trauma symptoms. All trauma therapies have an exposure element, during which the client focuses on the image and experience of the traumatic event. One of the best and most researched trauma therapies is EMDR, in which the client focuses on sensations, thoughts, images, and emotions connected to the trauma while following a quickly moving hand or pointer back and forth across the visual field. With both the prefrontal cortex and the amygdala stimulated, the brain begins to realize "It's now! The bad stuff is over!" and the trauma fades.

Somatic therapies, wedded with here-and-now awareness, are often helpful. The dual attention is often the focus on the sensations and muscle tension in the here-and-now body, while the client focusses on the trauma and the movement needed to successfully complete the undone reaction in the original trauma. The client is coached to mentally and physically push the attacker away (slowly, with full attention to the sensations) or swim up to the surface or reach out to the absent parent while feeling the emotions and sensations.

Ego state therapy, with its inherent creation of a dual attention (the trauma versus the right now adult), can heal simple trauma and is a necessary component of work with complex trauma. Here's an example of how it can work:

1. Solidify the here-and-now part of your client's strengths by having them imagine a role or an activity in which the client has felt strong, competent, protective, or nurturing—whichever is needed for this session (Korn & Leeds, 2002).
2. Have the client's here-and-now part identify the part that's stuck in the trauma.
3. Have the here-and-now part reach into the past, grab hold of the willing traumatized part and pull that traumatized part into the present time and place.
4. Have the client's present part orient the past part to its present, safe environment.
5. Check back for left over trauma. Pull through new trauma or the same trauma again, as many times as necessary, until the trauma is gone.
6. Hug the younger part inside (Shapiro, 2016).
7. (This technique includes some EMDR-based resource installation [Leeds, 2009], some Life Span Integration time travel [Pace, 2007], and some of my own modifications to each.)

For example: A young man went swimming in a lake at night. He'd had a few beers, and in the dark water, he got disoriented. Unable to tell which way was up, he thrashed around, until he

> "All trauma therapies have an exposure element, during which the client focuses on the image and experience of the traumatic event."

inhaled too much water and went limp. When he floated up to the surface, his friends grabbed him, did CPR, and got him breathing again.

Two weeks later, after nightmares, constant flashbacks, uncontrollable anxiety, and the inability to get into a running shower or a bathtub, he came to therapy. After the paperwork and assessment were complete (a bright, functional grad student, not otherwise traumatized or dissociative, ready to go) the therapist said, *"What's the most functional, strong part of you?"*

"When I'm running. I do distance and I'm really good."

"So, think about a time when you were ahead of the pack, full of energy, knowing you were going to nail that race."

"Got it."

"Feel the strength in your body. Connect with awareness that you're strong and in control."

"Go."

"I want that strong, sure part of you, that's right here in this room, to reach back two weeks and find that part of you that was drowning in the lake."

"Shit! Do I have to?" (Avoidance of the trauma is a hallmark of PTSD.)

"Yes, if you want to get over these flashbacks."

"Okay."

"You got that strong runner here? Good. Now reach back into the water and find that drowning guy. What do you notice in your body when you're with him?"

"Panic!"

"Feel that, and with your strong runner self, pull that guy to the surface and up through the last two weeks, all the way to right here and right now. . . Got him right here? Give him a towel, he's dripping on my floor! Let him know that he made it, and you're safe now. Good. . . Now go back to that lake again and see if there's any part of you still stuck there. There is? What's the feeling now?"

"Still some fear, but not as bad."

"Grab that part of you again, pull him out of there and out of that time, all the way up to right here and right now. Show him that you lived and you're here. . . And let's do another round. Strong runner, go back there and check. What's the feeling now?"

"Mad that the whole thing happened."

"Feel that anger in your body. Got it? Good. Grab that guy and get him out of the water, out of the people pounding on his chest, and all the way through those two weeks until now. Show this piece of you around your current, not-drowning life. He's here? Good. Another round. When you go back two weeks to that night at the lake, what do you notice now?"

"He's not there anymore."

"What's the feeling you notice?"

"I'm like, grateful, that I lived, and that my friends took care of me. And that I feel better now."

"Try this: think about taking a shower now. What do you notice?"

"No fear. Looking forward to the hot water, and finally getting really clean."

This is the rare best-case scenario: no early trauma, a bright and articulate not-too-avoidant client with a one-time event and the ability to hold the "dual attention" of his currently safe self and the drowning self from his past. Most trauma is more complex and takes more work to clear.

Exposure therapy (EX) finds a way to have clients write about or remember the trauma while keeping their attention in the room. There are many forms. Some involve relaxed states pendulating with the trauma memory (Wolpe, 1958). Some skip the relaxation and go into full-on "distress tolerance" by continual focus on the traumatic event (Foa, Hembree, & Rothbaum, 2007). Therapists may use virtual reality, writing, or simply remembering. Without the strong dual attention of EMDR, somatic therapy, or ego state therapy, EX sometimes exacerbates trauma symptoms and dissociation. Many EX clients drop out. (For example: For years, therapists at an agency that allowed only exposure therapy would clandestinely refer me clients who couldn't tolerate the exposure therapy, but were able to clear their trauma with the EMDR, somatic, and ego state therapies that I offered. Eventually, the therapists got training in methods other than exposure therapy and stopped sending me their clients. I hope you are never caught in this dilemma!)

Many therapies are great for supporting clients who have had trauma, but they don't make the trauma go away. Cognitive therapies help clients understand traumatic reactions and teach good self-talk to cope with it, but they do not transform it. Saying "I'm safe now; it's over" is true, but not the same as deleting flashbacks, anxiety, and nightmares. Psychodynamic therapies aid understanding and boost the client's ability to connect with and absorb emotional support, but they often don't vanquish the symptoms of PTSD. Both cognitive and psychodynamic therapies can come in handy when treating more complex trauma with attachment components. Neither regularly wipes out the trauma on its own.

Treating Complex Trauma

When the trauma or the attachment snafu occurs early and often—or later, but on and on for years—people's brains lay down wide neural highways of reaction to the subsequent, overwhelming emotions. When triggered by current situations or emotions, clients reflexively shift into their earlier trauma-time states or into their later coping ones. What might you see?

- **Spacing out.** What do you do? Gently say, *"Come back. Connect right here and now with me. You and I will hold that feeling together"* and *"What was that feeling you had right before you went away?"* or *"Feel inside for the feeling that sent you away."*
- **Needy young parts.** *"Let's get that adult you (the ANP) back in the room to help hold these little ones who really need a loving adult around. I'll coach you on the best ways to hold them. And if you don't want to hold them, let's put them in the healing place we imagined with the best caregiver we can imagine. This caregiver will hold them, play with them, feed them, and guard them every moment that you are awake, and every moment that you are asleep. As these kid parts of you are responded to every moment, they will*

start to know that they are loveable, loved, safe, and adorable—exactly what we wish they could have learned the first time around."

- **Angry, defensive parts who don't want to have anything to do with this stupid therapy that's bringing up the terrible feelings.** *"Notice I'm right here with you and your anger. It makes sense that you don't want to feel this stuff. Who would? I'm right here to help you build up your feeling muscles to hold this stuff and then get rid of it, forever. For right now, feel the anger and feel the old stuff and the big feelings that set them off."*

- **Totally dissociated parts (DID/tertiary dissociation).** When the client turns to you on the fifth session and says, "Who are you?" and "Where is this?" (and they're not demented), the client has reached the "Oh, s—t!" moment of therapy, which also means your client most likely has dissociative identity disorder. If this happens, you need to (re)introduce yourself and your function briefly, find out who and what age the presenting part of your client is, tell them that you will definitely talk to them later, and then tell them, authoritatively, *"At the count of three, I will snap my fingers and the part of you that came into the room at the beginning of the session will reappear. 1, 2, 3, [snap!]"* And when the part of the client you know reappears, ask *"Do you know what just happened?"* They often don't, and then you're both off on a new therapeutic path.

It will take months to years of work to get the ANPs/front people/hosts of your client with DID to recognize, connect to, and orient all the EPs/kid parts/alters to the present. It will take months to years to work through the trauma and abandoned affect held in each EP while new EPs continue to arise. And you will gently, slowly, assist in the full or partial integration of the parts.

An explanation of the full treatment of clients with DID is beyond the scope of this book If you just got your first DID client, get immediate consultation and help. Join the International Society for the Study of Trauma and Dissociation, take their online course (www.isst-d.org), and see if there is a member you can consult with. Read *Treating Trauma-Related Dissociation* (Steele, Boon, & van der Hart, 2017), my *Easy Ego State Interventions* (Shapiro, 2016), and everything else you can find. Steele and colleagues (2011) also wrote *Coping with Trauma-Related Dissociation*, which is good for clients and for therapists; it is full of worksheets and has clear explanations.

STRUCTURAL DISSOCIATION

PRIMARY DISSOCIATION
One Bad Event (PTSD)
Splint into **Trauma Symptoms** vs. **"Normal Self"**

SECONDARY DISSOCIATION
Many Traumas/Attachment Issues
You split between Neural Pathways for

Panic, Freeze	**Normal Function**
Fight, Flee, Cling	
Shutting down (Shame, Comply, Go Limp, Paralysis)	

TERTIARY DISSOCIATION (DID)
Early Traumas & Attachment Disasters

Safety (Protector) Fight, Flee, Cling	**Normal Function** (Parent, Worker, Spouse, Nurturer)
Shut Down (Victim) Shame, Comply, Limp	2 or more
Different Ages	
Parts of Traumas (Emotions, Sensations, Thoughts, P.O.V.)	

From *Visual Aids for Psychotherapy* (Shapiro, 2011)

12 / **Suicidal Clients**

Suicidal clients cannot stand what they're feeling. They can't see an end to the pain. They see only one way out. However, they are alive and in your office. Some piece of them wants to find a different way through the emotions. You have two jobs: Help them protect their lives until they can see a way to live. And help them through their pain and their beliefs about themself or the world that stand in the way of living.

Prevalence

According to the Centers for Disease Control and Prevention (2016), suicide was the tenth leading cause of death in the United States, claiming the lives of nearly 45,000 people in 2016. It was the second leading cause of death among individuals between the ages of 10 and 34, and the fourth leading cause of death among individuals between the ages of 35 and 54. Many of these people never sought therapy. The population with steepest rise in completed suicide are males who use guns in their attempt and who live in less populated northern states, where there is limited, if any, access to mental health services.

According to the National Institute of Mental Health (2019):

- Risk factors include prior attempts, a family or personal history of mental or substance disorder or violence, exposure to another person's suicide, sexual trauma, loss, and incarceration. Other factors include PTSD, poor attachment, poor social connectedness, and "difference" from cultural expectations (income, disability, ethnicity, sexual orientation or gender identity, victim of bullying).
- Suicidal ideation may occur with any diagnosis but is most prevalent in people with depression and people on the dissociative spectrum, from PTSD to personality disorders to DID. Bipolar disorder and psychotic disorders often generate suicidal thoughts, feelings, and behaviors.
- Women attempt suicide three times more frequently than men. Four times as many men die by suicide, mostly because they use guns. Fifty percent of all suicides involve a firearm that was present in the home.
- The rate of suicide for the 14- to 25-year-old demographic is rising sharply and is attributed to the social isolation, bullying, and lack of sleep that result from the increasing time these individuals spend on the Internet.

The Adverse Childhood Experiences Study was a 30-year-long study that tracked people's physical and mental health and related it to specific events that happened in their lives or to them before their 18th birthday. Adverse childhood experiences (ACE) included growing up in a house 1) with physical abuse, 2) with emotional abuse, 3) with sexual abuse, 4) in which someone was imprisoned, 5) in which the mother was beat up, 6) with an addict, 7) with a depressed, suicidal, or mentally ill person, or 8) in which a biological parent was lost, for any reason. Each person scored received one point for each adversity they experienced before they turned 18. An ACE score of 6 or more correlated with a 30-fold increase in attempted suicide (Felitti et al., 1998).

Triggers

There are many possible triggers for suicidal ideation, including:

- Depression, especially chronic depression
- Loss of job, status, pride, people, groups, health
- PTSD
- Overwhelming affect: shame, anger, hopelessness, grief, anxiety
- Mania
- Alcohol or drug use reduces inhibition of suicidal thoughts, or for addicts, the substance might be the reason—70% of attempted suicides are alcohol or drug related

Notice how many of the above are affect-related. Most suicide attempts are enacted to "manage" overwhelming emotions, whether from loss, PTSD, or mania.

Assessment

When assessing clients for suicide risk, listen carefully to your client and listen carefully to your own gut. Clients may deny thoughts or plans of killing themselves due to shame or because they want to keep the option of suicide open. Dissociative clients may have parts that don't know about the suicidal ideation or plans of other parts. If you know your client well, and know yourself well, and the hair on the back of your neck keeps rising, persist in your questions.

Questions at the Intake

- *"Have you ever thought about killing yourself?"*
- If yes, *"Have you ever attempted suicide? . . . Tell me about that."*

- Or, *"What kept you from trying?"*
- *"Are you having suicidal thoughts at the moment?"*

Questions for Currently Suicidal Clients

- *"Are they thoughts that you should be dead, that you're worthless, or a feeling that you can't stand, or something else?"*
- *"Do you have a plan?"*
- *"Do you have the means?"* (Use this question if the plan involves a gun, drugs, or another unusual way. Consider the lethality of the means.)
- *"What is keeping you alive right now?"* (Attachment to other people, goals, knowing that the feeling will pass?)
- *"How much of you wants to be dead? How much of you wants to be alive?"* (If they say that all of them wants to be dead, ask them what part of them got them to therapy that day.)

Chronic Suicidal Ideation

Some of your clients have lived for years with the idea of suicide. Most of these clients have had poor attachment and/ or early abuse. They hold the beliefs that they're not love-able, they should never have been born, and they have only been a burden. Borderline personality-disordered, or even more dissociated clients, may have states or parts stuck back in the experience of abuse, neglect, or hopelessness. Some dissociated clients may have parts or voices demanding "Kill yourself!" It's important to examine these feelings, parts, or voices and identify the time and place from which they arose. Ego state

"When assessing clients for suicide risk, listen carefully to your client and listen carefully to your own gut."

therapy, facilitating communication between the present-oriented parts and the younger, suicidal ones, is helpful for these clients.

Signs of Acute Suicidality

- There's an imminent plan.
- Client reports that it's hopeless, or they're hopeless and are too miserable to live.
- Client says, "No one can help, I'm just here to say good-bye."
- Client says good-bye or thank you out of the blue. (Case example: A client with DID, who had been stable and out of therapy for years, called me and told me that she wanted to thank me for all the good work that we'd done and that I'd made a big difference in her life. My response, *"If you're not in my office in one hour, I'm going to call the police to come get you and take you to the hospital."* She said, "How did you know?" I said, *"I know you and got scared the minute you thanked me."* It turned out that she was about to be evicted from her low-income apartment, and her younger parts wanted to "protect her" by killing the body, so they wouldn't have to move. We worked through that. She moved. And she's still around, many years later.)
- Client is giving things away.
- Client looks agitated, manic, extremely depressed, or unusually cheerful.
- Client comes in high for the first time.

Interventions

It's important to note that most people who attempt suicide and fail are glad to be alive. A study of people who survived after jumping off San Francisco's Golden Gate and Bay bridges showed that most were happy to be alive days, six months, and one year later (Rosen, 1975). It is in your client's best interests, and yours (since your state code most likely demands it), that you intervene in whatever way is necessary to keep your clients alive.

"Most people who attempt suicide and fail are glad to be alive."

Imminent Threat

When clients are acutely suicidal and don't think they can keep themselves safe, it's necessary to find them a safe place, with safe people, away from all means of suicide. Here are some scenarios and what you might do.

- Client calls and tells you that they've taken an overdose and are just saying goodbye.
  - Keep them on the phone as long as possible.
  - Call or text 911 for an ambulance and the police (to knock down the door, if necessary) to get your client. In this case, you may need to walk to a coworker's door, get them out of a session, and write them a note of what to do. It's okay. It's life or death.

- Client calls and says, "I am on the ledge/holding the gun/noose/pills." You say, *"What part of you called me? That's the part of you that wants to live . . . What part wants to die? How old is that part? . . . What triggered it this time? . . . And the part that wants to live, how old is that part?"* (usually more adult) . . . Connect with them. Show you care. Be careful! If a gun is involved, and you send in the police, it may trigger the suicide or the shooting of either the client or the police. Better to make a safety plan: get them to dump the means of suicide and to go to the ER, a friend's house, or a meeting, or to come straight to your office. Then make less immediate and longer term plans.

- Client is in your office and can't promise you that they won't harm themselves once they've left.
  - Assess their options: Go to a hospital? Is there a good friend, supportive family member, or church group who will put them up?
  - If a hospital is being considered, make sure it's a good option. If there are no psych wards in town, or if the facilities and support are completely inadequate, you may want to choose other options. (In Seattle, they may tie down a suicidal patient in an emergency room hallway for 24 to 48 hours. Not a good option!) If a client goes to the hospital, it's helpful to send someone along, a friend or family member, who can advocate for them. And they must go if there is no other way to make sure that they will live to heal another day.
  - You, or the client, contact the chosen option within the therapy session and arrange for:
    - A place to stay with good people. (Best case scenario: they pick the client up from your office.)
    - Disposal of the means from the plan (guns, pills, noose, etc).
    - The next clinical steps
      - Phone calls?
      - Next-day session(s)?
      - Medication review?

- Client can leave safely now, but you are unsure whether they can stay safe and alive.
  - Arrange, from the session, for someone else to meet them and take away the means (gun, noose, pills, etc.). People who can't use their planned method often don't use another.
  - Within the session, make a plan of who they will be spending time with (folks at AA meetings, church congregation, friends, family, etc.).
  - Warn them against drug or alcohol use because it can remove all kinds of inhibitions, including those to suicide.

- Write up a plan for their survival that includes interim support, a date and time for their next session, how they will spend their time, and what they will do—and a promise to do it—if they become overwhelmed and want to commit suicide, such as
  - Call 911 or the local crisis intervention clinic
  - Call you
  - Take themselves to the hospital

  The plan includes what you will be doing: extra sessions; more phone availability during the acute suicidal phase; a hospital visit, as a guest, since you're not a physician and don't have admitting privileges.
- You and the client both sign the safety plan. (This helps lock the client into the contract and covers your legal liability, in case there is a suicide.) I always shake hands on the contract, too, which is more personal and may promote more adherence.
- Keep tabs on the client.
  - If the client will be hospitalized, get a release to talk to staff about treatments and to plan the eventual release.
  - Be available for more text or phone connections, but set some limits to take care of yourself.
  - If the client will be with friends, get a release from the client that permits you to legally talk to one or two of them in case they sense a downturn.

- Client reports, "I almost killed myself this weekend!"
  - *"What kept you from doing following through? . . . What part of you wanted to? . . . What triggered it? . . . How do you feel about being here with me now? What did you learn this weekend about getting through this? . . . What do you want to remember when you get triggered again? . . . How can you connect with the wants-to-live part of you, no matter what you're feeling?"*
  - Implement a safety plan: contact with other people, ditch the method, schedule structured activities, decide what they should

do if the urge comes again, no booze agreement, contact the therapist. Here's an example of one I've written with a client:

"I_____ agree that most of me wants to stay alive and feel better. And that some of me wants to die when I am feeling hard emotions. And that I will stay alive for the parts of me that want to have a future. I will stay with Suzi, let her give me my daily pills, go for a walk with Ron every day, and call the Crisis Center if I can't get hold of [therapist]. [Client's Signature, Date] And that [therapist], agrees to see me for up to two (2) sessions weekly, keep her cell phone on when she's not in session or asleep, and do everything she knows to help heal the distress and build a stronger, happier me. [Therapist's signature, Date.]"

- A generic agreement includes the client agreeing to staying alive, using crisis intervention services if necessary, and the therapist agreeing to support the client through it.

- "I've got a fatal disease. I don't want to live through all the losses and pain of the disease. I'm ready to go."
  - Support the client to feel everything about the losses, to feel the fear, and to see what they can do to minimize pain and distress.
  - Understand that, whatever your beliefs, it's not your business to make the client's decision.
  - Help the client to distinguish between being truly ready to go and being overwhelmed with affect. You might say, *"I don't have a problem with you hastening the end. However, I'd like to help you look at what it means to be alive right now.*
    - *What things do you want do and which people do you need to connect with before you go?*
    - *If you could be pain-free, would you be willing to stay around for a while? Hospice or palliative care is all about keeping you comfortable, not prolonging life.* (Hospice is the cessation of

trying to cure the patient, with an emphasis on maximum pain control, dignity, and support by doctors, nurses, and social workers.)

- *I want you to make this decision with your best mind, not when you just got the diagnosis and are in shock. Can we work on getting calmer, so that you can think more clearly? I'm here to support whatever decision you make.*
- *Is there anybody in your life that you want to include in this decision?*

Many people who are suffering medically keep suicide as an option, but they don't use it if they are kept comfortable throughout their final days. Some states have assisted-suicide laws. Generally, patients must have a sign-off from two physicians, have a fatal disease, be cogent, and endure a two-week waiting period before they can receive the medication for the task. Other people stockpile medication they would need to do the deed. If people discuss this option with their families and let them know that they are going to take this option, it can reduce family members' shock, guilt, and anger at the person's death.

Working with Survivors of a Suicide by a Family Member or Friend

"My spouse/child/friend committed suicide. It's my fault! I should have known! I should have stopped it!"

- *"Tell me how you found out. Let's clear the trauma of that horrible moment."*
- *"You're in the shock part of grief now. During this part, you feel like it can't have happened, and your body is mobilized to do something. Your body is telling you that you must stop it, therefore you must have been*

able to. Let's hang out with the horrible truth: You weren't there. You didn't know. And they killed themself. They're dead . . . And notice what you're feeling now . . . Notice the difference between wishing you could have stopped it, and your actual ability to stop it. . . . Feel that awareness that they didn't involve you and did take their own life . . . What do you notice now? . . . Good, the tears are here. The grief is coming . . . When you circle back to blaming yourself, go back to 'I didn't know. I couldn't know. They're really gone. And what else am I feeling?'"

Countering "They'll be better off without me."

People with a lot of shame are likely to tell you that their family and friends will be happier when they, the client, are dead. I have heard parents of young children say that, and I counter it forcefully.

"If you kill yourself, you will fuck up your children for the rest of their lives. They will constantly tell themselves that they should have done something. They will tell themselves that you didn't love them enough to stay alive, which means that they aren't in any way loveable. Statistically, they will be 20 times more likely to commit suicide than they are now.

"It's important to directly confront the client's projection of not mattering to other people."

Kids learn from what you do, not what you say. If you kill yourself, you are showing them that life is not worth living; that emotions can't be changed; and that there is no hope. Is this what you want them to believe?

If we can keep you alive for now, until this horrible feeling and horrible idea passes, you will be doing your children, your friends, and your family a huge service. Let's figure out how to do that."

I use all the other interventions, and I think it's important to directly confront the client's projection of not mattering to other people, especially when children, even adult children, are involved.

Ritually-Abused Dissociative Identity Disordered Clients with Chronic Suicidal Ideation

These are some of the hardest and most suicidal cases I've worked with or consulted about. Many of them have suffered horrific abuse from multiple people. The abuse was often done to create dissociation, and to create introjects of the perpetrators' beliefs, instructions, and voices. They often have dozens of parts, many of them created on purpose. By the time I see these clients, they have often had many hospitalizations, many diagnoses, and many suicide attempts.

Therapy, in the beginning, includes ferreting out the parts that were programmed to die, and the parts that want to die in order to protect themselves from pain and danger, figuring out the internal and external triggers for suicide, and attempting to get the present-oriented, more adult, wanting-to-live parts in control. Here are questions I would often ask these clients, that can work for any dissociative client:

- *What part or parts of you are telling you this? Tell me about them.*
- *How old are these parts?* (Often young.)
- *How did they get the message that they shouldn't exist?* (In DID, often from abuse and neglect by parents or from a programmed message from organized abuse.) *What was happening then?*
- *Are there other parts of you that want to be alive? Tell me about them.*
- *What does your most grown up adult think about it.*

- *What can that adult tell those other parts? . . . Can you show these parts who is in your life now? What kind of support you have now? . . . Can you bring that/those kid(s) up here and show them the kinds of messages you get now from people?*
- *Who do you want in charge, the young* (state the age) *suicidal part of you, or your* (current age) *adult? . . . How can your adult keep those kids cared for, contained, and safe, and stay alive until we meet again?* (Then we would make a plan.)

It may take years to completely round up the suicidal parts. In these clients there may be "time-bombs", tied to dates, holidays, or birthdays, during which a seemingly stable client is triggered, by an abusive introject, to attempt suicide. It's been helpful to warn the oldest-wisest parts of these clients to watch out for this, and be ready to say, "No! Our life is better now and we want to live!" I've been thanked by clients, after many years of therapy, and, sometimes many suicide attempts or rounds of intense ideation, for helping them stay alive to enjoy a stable, safe, and enjoyable present life.

Bullied Teenager

Joan was 15, a "big feeler" with a high-strung body, and in therapy to deal with her ever-present anxiety. Her emotions always showed in her expressions and her tendency to blush, which made her an easy target for bullies. Other kids enjoyed the power of making Joan blush, cringe, or cry.

One day, she came into session determined that suicide was the only way to deal with it. "They're never going to leave me alone! I can't stand it! I'm done!" She had a plan: jumping. And it was to be a "fuck you" suicide, with a note to all the people who had harassed her.

Knowing that teenagers often don't have an idea of the future, I directed her to consider both choices, dying or living: *"What happens if you go off that bridge?"* "I'll be really scared for a minute, and then I'll be dead." *"What happens if you're dead?"* "Nothing. I'll be gone and they'll never hurt me again." *"So, what happens if you choose to live."* "Those assholes will win, and they'll keep bothering me." *"And then what?"* "I don't know. I'll stay alive and stay in school." *"And then what?"* "Eventually, I'll graduate, and get away from those assholes." *"And then what?"* "I'll go to college, or maybe an art school." *"And then what?"* "I'll probably get a job in my field and a relationship." *"Do you think that future person will be happy?"* "Definitely!" *"I want you to hold "dead" in one hand and 23, working, loving, and happy in the other. Which seems like the better choice?"* "Being 23 and working and loving!" *Would you like me to help you get there?* "Yes!" *"Where inside do you feel that 'Yes'?"* She points to her heart and belly. *"In the meantime, would you like to make a plan to stay alive so that those insecure assholes won't win?"* "Absolutely!"

The plan was to 1) Feel everything, despite their taunting. 2) Retort with "At least I have a heart!" or "You must be really insecure to resort to bullying." 3) Post articles about the insecurity of bullies in her social media (after reading them herself). 4) Contact me or someone appropriate if she ever had the suicidal feelings again. 5) Keep working on anxiety and shame in therapy . . . She did all of these things!

Attachment-Disordered Client After Breakup

Tom was 39, had alcoholic parents who were cold and critical, and had struggled to get through college, find work, and connect with others. He had been in an intense relationship for three years with a woman who alternately adored him and hated him. One day, telling Tom "You are the worst thing that ever happened to me," she abruptly broke up with him.

At our next session, Tom told me that, after finding homes for his dogs and writing a will, he planned to kill himself. "I have nothing to live for. I'm a complete failure at everything. There's no reason for me to be here anymore . . . I can't stand it."

My first thought was *he doesn't have any space or tolerance for his grief.* So, instead of talking about suicide, I went right to his affect: *"I'm so sorry that you've lost her! Let's see if we can let some of that grief out."* I sat close, looked into his eyes, and told him to feel the tears behind his eyes and to breathe into the tightness in his chest. *"You're really going to miss her!"*

Within minutes he was sobbing. Each time he tried to stop, or turn away, I told him to look at me and that I welcomed everything he was feeling. After about 15 minutes, Tom began to naturally come to a calmer place. We discussed the grieving process, and how hopelessness was a normal part of it. And we discussed how his family didn't equip him to be able to feel it all and let it move through.

Then we talked about his suicidal ideation:

> *"Are you thinking about suicide right now?"*
> "I'm feeling better. And it doesn't seem like the only way."
>
> *"What do you need to do stay alive?"*
>
> "What you said, 'Feel it all.' And I need to hang out with other people; and the dogs."

We continued to discuss his self-care plans and what to do if the suicidal ideation returned. We made a safety plan:

"If I am thinking of killing myself:

1. I will notice what I'm feeling, breathe deeply, see what the feelings are, and whether I need to cry again.
2. If that doesn't calm me, I'm going to call Robin, and if she's not around, I'll call the Crisis Clinic.
3. I'll make a plan to be around Bob or Susan. And today, I'm going to let them know that I may be asking to hang out with them.
4. If all else fails, I'll take myself to the Emergency Room.
5. I promise to follow this plan, and Robin promises to support me through all these emotions until I don't need this plan anymore."

We both signed and dated the plan, and then shook hands on it. Therapy, for several weeks, included the full range of grief-related affect: anger, sadness, hopelessness. The suicidal ideation came and went, but he did not go so far as to develop a plan. We worked with earlier losses and childhood affects, which boosted his here-and-now functioning. The suicidal ideation lifted, though some normal sadness remained.

13 / **Treating Anxiety**

Anxiety drives many people to therapy and is a part of many diagnoses. It can be mild and situational, genetically wired in, secondary to trauma, and/or crippling, keeping people isolated and avoidant of some or all activities and of learning new things.

Of course, anxiety isn't all bad. Think of the times you've left your home and anxiety arose as you walked out the door, along with the realization that you've left your phone/wallet/work on the table. Anxiety, hopefully, gave you an important signal to grab your needed stuff before you were too far away. Anxiety keeps us from doing dangerous things. It can alert us to something or someone being "off" in our environment before our front brains have registered it. Gavin de Becker (1997) wrote *The Gift of Fear and Other Survival Signals that Protect Us from Violence*, which talks about the usefulness of anxiety in keeping us safe. He advocates that we carefully scan the environment or the people around us when we feel the internal alarms to ensure our safety.

However, it is a problem when generalized anxiety keeps our clients from sleep, new activities, or from leaving the house; when it creates endless circles of nonsensical thoughts, or repetitive behaviors (OCD); or when it creates panic reactions to relatively harmless things (phobias).

Diagnosing Anxiety

Four ways to look at anxiety, which are by no means mutually exclusive:

1. The client was born with an anxious, hair-trigger nervous system, is a "highly sensitive person" (Aron, 1996) with more awareness of affect and actually stronger affect, and may have another diagnosis, such as bipolar disorder, autism, or ADHD, that includes anxiety.
2. The client experienced trauma that gave them PTSD or another trauma-related diagnosis, of which anxiety is a part.
3. The client lives or has lived in an unsafe world, in which anxiety is or was a useful, understandable response.
4. The client has physical condition or takes a medication that creates anxiety: some possible culprits are hyperthyroidism, certain antidepressants, or too much ADHD medication. If someone has no history of anxiety or trauma, is not about to take a huge test or perform in front of thousands, and is in an unrelentingly anxious state, a physical examination and medication review may be order.

The first kind of client can be easy to spot. Many fit my diagnosis of "skinny, nervous person": angular, hyper-aware of every sound and change in the environment, quick to react, and encompassing a wide range of strong feelings. Not all have that body shape, but all have sensitive neurological wiring. When you do your intake, ask who else in the family has/had anxiety. With this kind of client, you may find inherited sensitivity, bipolar, or other mood disorders running through a quadrant, or more, of the family. Then ask them about their responses to stimuli: *How are you in loud environments? How do you react to changes in temperature? Were you an anxious kid? Did you have any big fears or phobias when you were little? Do you have any now? Are there any activities you'd like to do that you avoid? Do you worry what other people think about you?*

The second kind, PTSD clients, will report that they were just fine until the assault/accident/military stint/bullying occurred and that they've been anxious ever since. Your job with them will be clearing the trauma out of their nervous systems and reintroducing them to the sense of here-and-now safety. Check their entire trauma history, since recent traumatic reactions may be exacerbations of old distress. It helps to understand that people with PTSD may have been misdiagnosed with anxiety disorders. With these people, it's delightful to clear the trauma and watch the anxiety completely disappear.

The third kind, the people who have had to be watchful or who live in unsafe circumstances (homeless, person of color, transsexual or transgender, in prison, scary and abusive family, etc.), can be helped to distinguish between what's safe and what's not and when to let their guard down. Sometimes, awareness, respite, and acceptance are the best we can offer. The ones who are no longer in the chronically bad situation will take some time to move it out of their bodies and brains.

Anxious Bodies

Get complete family histories. Find out who else in the family has anxiety, bipolar disorder, or depression. (Depression can be a bodily reaction to too much anxiety.) Find out if your clients are "highly sensitive people" and need to read Elaine Aron's (1996) book about them to normalize their big responses to every stimulus. Have they always had big reactions to changes of temperature, crowds, noise? Are they exhausted by too much input? Can loud music be physically painful to them? Or do they simply have bodies that are easily triggered into a mobilized fight-or-flight state (Porges, 2017)? You can often see the anxiety in their twitchy bodies and their big responses to every sound or thought. People with pale skin may flush easily. Eyes may snap open in alarm. Bodies may be held rigidly, in an attempt to control responses to external and internal stimulation. If that's the case, normalize their situation. *"It's not your fault you've got this. People are born with different kinds of bodies, and yours feels everything more strongly than about 78% of other people. That means that 22% of humans have bodies like yours. These sensitive bodies are more prone to this kind of problem. Luckily, we know what to do with you all."*

"Get complete family histories. Find out who else in the family has anxiety, bipolar disorder, or depression."

Find out what troubles them. Is it worry about everything (generalized anxiety); fits of out-of-control gasping and terror (panic attacks); worry about being acceptable (social anxiety); worry and avoidance of very particular things or situations (phobia); or repetitively coming back to one thought or behavior (obsessive–compulsive disorder); or some or all of the above?

Here are some questions to ask your anxious clients:

- Is your body usually anxious, even when things are going well? (generalized anxiety disorder [GAD])
- Do you have panic attacks?
- What do you worry about the most?
- Any phobias? (Common ones include heights [acrophobia], claustrophobia [enclosed places], airplanes [aviophobia], throwing up [emetophobia], social situations [anthrophobia], germs [mysophobia], and the sounds people make when eating [mysophonia])

- Are there obsessive thoughts when your body gets anxious? Do those thoughts ever get you to do things like check the door locks over and over? (obsessive–compulsive disorder [OCD])
- Is there one worry you have, over and over again? (OCD)
- What do you avoid doing?
- Are you able to do things, even though you're anxious about them? How do you do that?

Wired-to-be-anxious people need tools to get their bodies under some conscious control. Start with general advice and then get very specific. Find out how much caffeine they're consuming. I've solved three cases of GAD by having new clients wean themselves off of four or more double lattes a day. Have these clients wean off slowly, or they will have big headaches. A cup less every few days should do it.

Tools

Have your anxious clients use several tools to calm down. These are on a handout I give to clients:

Exercise

1. Get aerobic exercise: run, walk quickly, dance.
2. Yoga or Pilates will get you focused and in your body.

Meditate

Find and use your favorite online app or simply notice your breath, your body, your thoughts, and keep pulling your attention back to NOW.

4 x 4 x 4 Breathing

1. Breathe out slowly to a count of 4. Inhale slowly to a count of 4. Hold breath for 4 counts. Do 4 times.
2. To cure a panic attack: Breathe out all the way, then breathe in halfway. Do eight times.

Silencing the Alarm

Feel where the anxiety is in your body. Put the heel of your right hand on your left eyebrow, near the nose. Brush your hand from your nose to behind your ear and down your neck to the tip of your shoulder. Flatten your hand and brush from your shoulder, past your elbow, and off the back of your left hand. Do this three times, then switch sides and do three more times. Keep doing sets until the anxiety disappears. (When I taught this exercise, which is based on acupuncture meridians, to a conference-full of psychotherapists in 2017, Stephen Porges, the famous researcher, told me that it works because it switches the vagus nerve from fight-or-flight to social-connection.)

Vagal Hold

Put your right hand on your heart and your left on your belly. Breathe deeply for at least ten minutes.

Beauty Awareness

Look around and notice anything that pleases your eye. Keep your attention right there for a minute. Find something else that is pleasant to look at. Keep looking around for what pleases you and notice what happens.

Gravity and Grounding

Notice gravity holding you in your chair. Lift different body parts and drop them. Imagine running a cord or a root from the bottom of your spine and from each foot, rooting you like a tree. Imagine breathing down the cords into the ground.

Sending and Receiving Love

Imagine breathing into and from your heart. Imagine the people you love. Send love out of your heart to everyone you love with each exhale. Bring love into your heart with each inhale. Breathe in love, breathe out love.

Two-Hand Technique

In one hand hold how scary the situation feels, and in the other, how dangerous it actually is. Hang out with that for a while, and explain to your body that it's okay to relax around this, and at the same time drop your shoulders, breathe deeply, and notice your safe surroundings.

I have clients practice the exercises while thinking about anxiety-provoking things. Then we imagine how and when they will use these tools in the real world. At the next session, we check in on the homework to see how it worked. These activities only work when people do them! Some clients will easily add these activities to their daily lives. Some will need a therapeutic push (or two or three) to add them to their daily schedules: *"When can you get your run in? Can you set an alarm on your phone that reminds you to turn on the app and meditate for ten minutes? Why don't you turn on your phone right now and find the schedule of that yoga class near your home/office?"*

EMDR clients will imagine doing these things in the future while receiving bilateral stimulation. Other people's clients will simply imagine doing them.

Obsessive-Compulsive Disorder

People with obsessive–compulsive disorder (OCD) generally fit the in the "born anxious" category and develop a nervous system reflex of

1. Feeling anxiety
2. Experiencing a repetitive thought (an unsuccessful attempt to combat the anxiety)
3. Developing a compulsive need to do something or prevent something tied to that thought

Some common themes among people with OCD:

- Germs are everywhere (true), and if I touch door handles/faucet handles/etc., I will die imminently (not true). I must never touch these things, and if I do, I must go through a long and hard ritual of cleansing.
- I just know that I'm going to throw my baby out of the window; I must never open the window, and I must worry about it repetitively.
- I must touch that spot on the wall every time I pass it, or something bad will happen.
- If I do _____, I must worry about it every minute, imagining all the ways it could fail.

All of these are futile defenses against anxiety that only make it worse. And it doesn't work to solely explain that to clients. Logic rarely works with anxiety disorders, since they don't arise from the logical part of the brain. You start with logic and move to direct confrontation of the anxiety.

Here is one process that can work:

> Start with the explanation: *Our brains are amazing in the way they try to fix the problem of anxiety. But they're not very good at it. Your body gets anxious and your brain says to you "Anxiety!*

There's a threat! I'm going to die! I must do something!" Then it lies to you about how to get safe. That's how you got into this ritual. We're going to break this ritual by directly changing the reflex. So, when you have these anxious thoughts or feel you have to do your compulsion:

1. Tell your brain that you know it's lying to you and to stop it! (Sprowls & Marquis, 2013)
2. Notice the anxiety in your body.
3. Ground yourself.
4. Breathe into your belly.
5. Look around and notice that you are physically safe.
6. Use your other relaxation tools.
7. Re-examine the thoughts as thoughts when your body is calmer. (Shapiro, 2018)

Walk through these steps with your client, having them imagine each trigger to the obsessive thought or behavior, telling the brain to stop it, and following the rest of the protocol. If you do EMDR, this is an excellent time to use bilateral stimulation. Otherwise, keep your connection up as you go through the steps together. Work through all the triggers. Then give these steps as homework. It may be helpful for the client to have a sheet with these instructions to take home, or a photograph of them on their phone, or an audio recording of you reading the steps.

"Consistently bring the client back to the safe present, a good connection with you, and a more relaxed body."

Don't expect an instant cure. Your client will still have an anxious body, and it's hard to make a reflex go away. Do expect your client to be able to identify anxiety as the problem and calming the body as the solution and to start doing calming exercises more frequently. I often ask clients how likely the OCD thought or behavior is to actually keep them safe: *Give me the percentage of times that this thought works to calm you down.* Or I suggest they hold *"If I ever touch a doorknob and don't immediately wash my hands for ten minutes, I'll die within a day!"* in one hand and *"what my rational mind knows"* in the other hand. Which one should you be listening to? (Shapiro, 2005)

Consistently bring the client back to the safe present, a good connection with you, and a more relaxed body. Then take them through a worst-case scenario: *Imagine you touched a doorknob with something sticky on it and there are no bathrooms open in which to wash up. And you forgot your hand sanitizer. And you just have to be with your sticky hand and the anxiety. Walk through how you're going to notice the thoughts as crazy thoughts, notice the anxiety shooting through your body, and use your tools to calm your body down.*

Phobias

Our nervous systems try to keep us safe by warning us to avoid perceived danger. Sometimes, usually in the wired-to-be-nervous people, our body/brain develops huge fear-and-avoidance responses to things that are not very dangerous. Some phobias occur as the result of a real scare: fear of flying after a scary plane ride, or fear of socializing after an unfortunate social encounter. Some seem to arise out of nowhere, such as misophonia, in which normal sounds (e.g., people chewing or sniffing or clicking pens) create huge fear-and-avoidance responses. I once worked with a boy who couldn't eat with his family and didn't want to live in a dorm because he'd have to hear people eating. It had arisen from disgust at some slurping sound and worsened from there. Many phobias arise from situations in which there is some possible danger (the elevator *could* get stuck; the plane *could* crash; there *could* be a death-causing bacterium on that doorknob), but often, as with misophonia, there is no possible or likely danger. You can use the same treatment with both possibly-dangerous and not-dangerous objects of phobia.

1. Identify the fear and when it started: *Did something happen, or did it arise out of nowhere?*
2. Explain phobias: *Your body feels huge anxiety and tries to protect you by telling you that it would be fatal to encounter this situation/thing.*
3. Then explain what's next: *Our job is to get you to notice the difference between fear of things that actually could kill you, like getting hit by a car, and the fear of feeling the fear of flying/hearing people slurp/going outside/being in the room with a spider. We're going to work first on getting you to tolerate the fear so it doesn't stop you, and then we'll get rid of it.*
4. As with OCD, you can bring up the triggering thing (exposure), have the client notice the fear and avoidance emotions and thoughts, and stay with them. EMDR is especially good at knocking down the distressing physical and cognitive reactions and is my treatment of choice in this phase. Otherwise, being with the affect, breathing, maintaining constant eye contact, and allowing the distress to move through can be good. I often get clients laughing in this phase, since it's hard to laugh and be terrified at the same time. After a while, the response lessens, and the phobia dims. Tell your clients to watch out for another phobia that may take its place and to use the same tools if it does.

Panic Attacks

Panic attacks are real and terrifying and are, in themselves, traumatic events. The body is in full flight-or-fight mode (unmyelinated ventral vagal state): breathing is disrupted, becoming fast gasps for air; the body may shake and sweat profusely; most of the thinking brain is off line except "RUN!"; and there is a sense of complete lack of control. When you treat people suffering from panic attacks, you have two goals: teaching them how to stop the attacks, and treating the PTSD (and often avoidance of perceived triggers) that ensues from living through them.

There are often no known triggers to this profoundly physical event, but there are ways to stop panic attacks from happening. Control is the issue, and these techniques give the control back to the conscious brain.

This is what I tell clients:

1. Force the lungs to slow down: *Breathe in half-way, breathe out all the way, all the way. Breathe in half-way, breathe out all the way. Continue until you calm down.* (This reverses the hyperoxygenation of the body that goes along with the gasping for breath.)
2. *Look around you and notice that you're safe.* (Orienting response.)
3. *Do the Silencing the Alarm exercise: brush your hand from your eyebrow to your ear, your neck, your shoulder, your elbow and off the top of your hand several times on each side.*
4. *Feel gravity holding you in your chair and holding your feet on the ground. You've still got gravity.*
5. *Drop your shoulders, look around again, and notice, as you keep breathing, that as you relax your body, you're dropping the panic.*
6. *And as you notice that, do the Vagal Hold: put your right hand over your heart and your left over your belly, and hold that for five minutes as you breathe in for a count of four, hold for four, breathe out for four, wait for four counts before the next inhale.*
7. *If those aren't working quickly enough, run in place—fast—to trick your body into thinking it got away.*

Clients can record your voice or their voice giving these instructions; they can take a picture of them or write them down. During a panic attack, people often don't have enough thinking brain to remember instructions, but they may remember that they *have* instructions that they can follow.

Once your clients are using these techniques to stop the cascade of panic, you can start looking for triggers. They are usually a shift in bodily state. For some people, relaxation itself is a trigger because they believe it's not safe to feel safe. For others, the trigger may be any anxious thought or upcoming event. Walk them through the situations and have them begin to practice various breathing and relaxation exercises before the attack can begin. Ask them at the beginning of each session if they've had occasion to use the techniques and how using them has worked. Often, you'll get tales of anxiety and relief. People are very happy to get control over their panic. (EMDR practitioners can knock down the anxiety with bilateral stimulation then focus on the future template of action.)

When clients are able to stop the attacks, ask how worried they are about the next attack. If they are showing signs of PTSD about possible future attacks or get caught up by memories of the worst ones, it's time to use trauma therapy on the memories of past attacks.

Performance Anxiety

People don't have to have a formal anxiety disorder to be nervous about doing well, looking good, or making a fool of themselves in front of others. As social animals, we are prone to worry about fitting in and about our place in the herd or hierarchy. People with anxiety disorders are more likely to have these fears. The treatment is similar for those with and those without formal anxiety disorders.

1. Distinguish between "fear" and "getting ready to go": *When we're about to do something big, our body pumps up the adrenalin to get us ready to go. What percentage of this feeling is fear and what percentage is pumping up?*
2. Identify the fear: *Doing well? Completely blowing it? Being acceptable?*

3. Identify the probability that the worst-case scenario will happen: *Likely? Impossible? 50%?*

4. Identify the likelihood it will turn out fine, and define success: *If you get through the job interview while keeping eye contact, answering the questions correctly, and showing your best face, was it successful, even if they pick another candidate?*

5. Identify what is within the client's control and what isn't: "I can control my preparedness for the interview by learning all I can about the corporation and the job I'm interviewing for" versus "I can't make them hire me."

6. Do the Two-Hand technique: *In one hand, hold the awareness that you know how to talk to bosses, you are good at your job, and people generally like you. In the other, hold the fear that you'll be unable to talk, you'll look like a fool, and you'll completely blow it. Which one is more likely?*

7. Then walk the client through the steps of doing the behavior, with the addition of all the calm-down techniques we've talked about before. Let them imagine the "pumped up" feeling as an energy source, not a warning of catastrophe. Have them imagine using that energy for whatever they're doing: *Of course you're worried about walking into the new class/social group/etc. It's new, you're a social animal/it's a new situation/your livelihood depends on this. Feel the anxiety, and feel the extra oomph that comes with prepping to do this thing. Let that new energy run through, and remember it's not about danger, it's about readiness. Are you ready? Great!*

Someone born with an anxious or more responsive body will likely have it forever. In fact with age, the myelin sheaths around our nerves start to fray and the body's responsiveness can increase. Some people may experience anxiety for the first time in their older age. Others may experience a general increase in anxiety. It's good to normalize the experience and provide tools for calming. Successful treatment for anxiety may not include the eradication of anxiety in the client. Unless the client has PTSD or situation-specific anxiety in a not-very-anxious body, they are likely to remain highly sensitive. At the conclusion of successful therapy, highly sensitive clients will not be obsessive or phobic and they will be somewhat calmer and have a set of tools to calm their anxious bodies, as needed.

14 / **Treating Addiction**

Imagine you haven't had any fluids for many hours. Imagine your body keeps sending you messages to drink something. When you think of a tall glass of water, the dopamine system in your body lights up, giving you feelings of pleasure. As you try to focus on other things, your body gives you more signals of distress. You keep thinking about water. You feel your parched mouth and throat. You start getting anxious and find it difficult to focus on anything else. When you finally drink that water, your body sends pleasure and reward signals throughout your brain and body. This is how our body and brain train us to do what we need to do to survive. And this mechanism can kick in to addict us to other substances and behaviors that can threaten our lives, our plans, and our functioning.

Whether people get addicted to psychoactive substances, food, or behaviors (gambling, sex or porn, video games, cutting), the mechanism is similar. Typically, an uncomfortable feeling arises and the drive to eradicate it reflexively kicks in, drawing the person toward an addictive substance or behavior. The driving feeling is usually anxiety or shame. If the person already uses physically addictive substances, the driving feeling could be from withdrawal symptoms. Either way, the biological reward systems kick in at the thought of the substance or behavior and gets even stronger every time the substance or behavior is used. The longer the addiction cycle runs, the more brain real estate it takes over, which is why long-standing addictions can be so hard to kick.

Imagine you were in a sealed room from which I was draining all the air. As the oxygen became scarcer, you would do anything to get the air back: you would bargain with and then threaten me, break a window, throw yourself against the door—you would do anything to live. That is the desperation many addicts feel when faced with losing their "fix."

Many businesses promote addiction. Obviously, companies that sell alcohol and nicotine stand to gain from "hooked" consumers. Consider the gambling industry; some of the drug companies that sell opiates; online games; porn sites. All these industries work hard to hook the dopamine systems of their consumers. Our job is to promote the conscious choices and health of clients over the profit of these companies.

Treating Addiction

Motivational Interviewing

No one wants to be an addict. Most people who are addicted to something know that what they're doing is harmful. Some are in denial—even *thinking* that they should stop goes against the built-up neural networks of addiction. Telling a client, *"You're an addict, and you need to stop this behavior now"* is useless. They either know it and can't stop, or they are in denial and will simply argue with you to protect their lifeline to feeling good/normal/happy/not desperate.

Motivational interviewing is a good way to work around this resistance and denial. You start by *engaging*, establishing a working relationship based on trust and respect. You move to *focusing* the client's direction, then *evoking*, which is eliciting the client's own motivations for change while inspiring hope and confidence. The last step is *planning*, which involves the client making a commitment to change and, with the therapist, developing a specific plan of action. Miller, Zweben, DiClemente, and Rychtarik (1992) provide this list of guidelines for motivational interviewing:

1. Motivation to change is elicited from the client, and is not imposed from outside forces.
2. It is the client's task, not the counselor's, to articulate and resolve their ambivalence.
3. Direct persuasion is not an effective method for resolving ambivalence.
4. The counseling style is generally quiet and elicits information from the client.
5. The counselor is directive, in that they help the client to examine and resolve ambivalence.
6. Readiness to change is not a trait of the client but a fluctuating result of interpersonal interaction.
7. The therapeutic relationship resembles a partnership or companionship.

"No one wants to be an addict. Most people who are addicted to something know that what they're doing is harmful."

A Motivational Interview

Below is an example of a motivational interview:

"Let's talk about what you like about the pot you're smoking. What are your favorite things about it?"
   "Well, it calms me down."

"What else do you like about it?"
   "It feels good. Everything just seems easier when I'm high."

"What else?"

"It gets me more present, not thinking about all my problems. And it's fun!"

"That makes total sense to me. There are a lot of positives around being high. Is there anything that's not working with pot?"

"Well, I'm not very motivated to get things done."

"Tell me more about that."

"I'd rather just watch a movie than clean up, or do my homework, or do anything goal-oriented."

"Anything else?"

"I'm not very social when I'm stoned. I don't really want to see anyone or do anything, even fun stuff with people."

"So, it's hard to get things done or get out to be with people. Anything else?"

"After a while, I get kind of depressed. I mean it feels good to get high, and then I kind of get stuck and then down. And I'm getting more isolated, the more I smoke."

"So, I'm hearing that pot is good for calming down and initially feeling really good and present. And that when you're high it's hard to get things done or to see people, and then you can get depressed from it. Am I getting this right?"

"Yeah, that's it."

"So, there's good stuff and bad stuff with it. Good at first, then not so good."

"Yeah."

"I'm thinking about dopamine. That's the chemical in our brain that turns on when we're thirsty and think about water, or we're hungry and see a good meal laid out. It gives us good vibes toward doing what's good for us. But sometimes it latches onto things that might have a mix of consequences. And it sounds like you get a big dopamine reaction when

you're thinking of smoking a joint. And then things shift, after a while, to not so good. Is that what you're experiencing?"

"I think so."

"Looking at it this way, what do you think?"

"I think that there's a problem."

"What's the problem?" (Notice the therapist isn't 'leading the witness'.)

"Pot feels good, but it's messing up my life. I'm not doing what I need to do, like getting stuff done and getting out of the house to see people."

"So, what are you thinking now?"

"I should quit. . . But what would I do when I feel bad? It makes me scared to give up something that helps me!"

"Would it make sense to quit if you don't have any other way to calm down or feel in the present moment?"

"Not really."

"Would it make sense to quit if you had other ways to calm down and feel present?"

"It could!"

After that discussion, there's permission to move forward. The therapist talks about calming and mindfulness techniques, reminds the client that it's not a solo endeavor and that the therapist is firmly in the client's corner, and they plan steps to learning new coping skills and weaning off marijuana. At one point the therapist asks how much money the client spends on pot, and they add that to the reasons it'll be good to quit. Never does the therapist tell the client what to do. Though, as in other good therapy, in motivational interviewing the therapist guides the process, and the decisions belong to the client.

Getting Clean

When somebody quits using marijuana, the fat-soluble THC lasts in the body for weeks; therefore, people don't have dangerous withdrawals and can wean off or quit completely without adverse physical effects. People who are addicted to alcohol, opiates, or other powerful drugs may experience horrible, and possibly dangerous or fatal, effects when they quit their substance. These people often need short-term hospitalization to taper them off or to medicate them while their bodies detox from the substance. Find the resources in your area for getting people through this first part of getting clean. There are some new medications for opiate addicts that can help them taper off their drugs of choice while staying "outside." Make sure you talk to a physician or an other detoxification expert before your client attempts stopping a powerful substance.

Some substances change the brain and body so much that it's nearly impossible for those addicted to them to survive getting off them, physically or emotionally, without medical and around-the-clock professional support. People who are addicted to opiates or methamphetamine and many who are addicted to alcohol need inpatient care to detox, to get through the panic a newly sober body experiences, and then to rewire their brain for sobriety. Look for a facility that is licensed in their state, takes the client's insurance, can do detoxification (if needed), has individual and group services, and can mesh with the work you're doing with your client. Ask if the facility has continuing support after the live-in treatment. Some offer intensive outpatient services that feature daily group and individual treatment, while allowing clients to live at home. Make sure the treatment staff are happy to talk to you, the therapist, before, during, and after your client's stint "inside."

Some treatment programs are based mostly on the twelve-step model (see below), while others deal directly with the underlying trauma, attachment, and affect issues. Look for a program that includes direct treatment for the whole client.

Twelve-Step Programs

If you're working with addiction, you should be familiar with the anonymous groups, their steps, and their language. Many people go to them and find help, support, fellowship, and, while they're there, gain the ability to eventually help others.

Twelve-step programs are volunteer-run fellowships that support recovery from a variety of addictive substances and compulsive behaviors, including Alcoholics Anonymous (AA; the first one), Narcotics Anonymous, Cocaine Anonymous, Gamblers Anonymous, and Sex and Love Anonymous. There are groups in nearly every town, often several days each week. With the help of a "sponsor" who has more recovery, group members work through a series of "steps." The twelve steps from Alcoholics Anonymous are:

> **"If you're working with addiction, you should be familiar with the anonymous groups, their steps, and their language."**

1. We admitted we were powerless over alcohol—that our lives had become unmanageable.
2. Came to believe that a Power greater than ourselves could restore us to sanity.
3. Made a decision to turn our will and our lives over to the care of God as we understood Him.
4. Made a searching and fearless moral inventory of ourselves.
5. Admitted to God, to ourselves and to another human being the exact nature of our wrongs.
6. Were entirely ready to have God remove all these defects of character
7. Humbly asked Him to remove our shortcomings.
8. Made a list of persons we had harmed, and became willing to make amends to them all.

9. Made direct amends to such people wherever possible, except when to do so would injure them or others.
10. Continued to take personal inventory and when we were wrong promptly admitted it.
11. Sought through prayer and meditation to improve our conscious contact with God as we understood Him, praying only for knowledge of His will for us and the power to carry that out.
12. Having had a spiritual awakening as the result of these steps, we tried to carry this message to alcoholics and to practice these principles in all our affairs. (Alcoholics Anonymous, 2019)

Reading through the twelve steps, you can see that many people, especially atheists, would immediately reject the Anonymous path. And there are many people who can commit to a "higher power" that isn't religious, such as the "power of the group." Other people don't like the group structure. And some don't like the long-term commitment. However, about half of the people who commit to the ongoing fellowship of AA and its related programs have long, if not perfectly abstinent, recoveries (Kelly & Yeterian, 2008). The good things about Anonymous groups:

1. They're everywhere.
2. They are built-in support groups. Many addicts' social lives are or were centered around substance use: partying, bars, selling drugs, gambling, frequenting prostitutes. Recovery groups provide places to go and people to be with who are no longer in the "life" and who are accessible in case of an emergency, and they can be immensely supportive of newcomers.
3. Members share knowledge of outside resources.
4. People don't feel alone in their addictions.
5. The price is right! It's free, in the beginning and people are asked, but not required to make a small donation.
6. People can "slip" and still be part of the group. "Falling off the

wagon" is normal. So is climbing back on. This is important, since many people will struggle before becoming abstinent.

7. For people who have an active spiritual life or a history of it, whatever concept of Higher Power they have is supported in the group.

But people can have problems with Anonymous groups:

1. The spiritual parts, though there is also AA for atheists and the concept of a "Higher Power" can be broad, are difficult for many people.
2. Not all groups are equal, and there may be problems due to the personalities in charge.
3. While it is anonymous, in a small town people may not be able to find a meeting that's separate from their other social groups.
4. Anonymous groups don't speak to the underlying causes of addiction: affect tolerance, trauma, and attachment issues. A few of them have actively discouraged psychotherapy as not "with the program," though most are supportive.

Psychotherapies for Addictions

CBT can be very helpful in rounding up the "stinking thinking" of many addictions. Newer CBT treatments may have a mindfulness component which is very helpful for addicts.

DBT was originally developed for work with clients with borderline personality disorder and is now used to help many addicts develop the affect tolerance and mindfulness that can keep them clean.

EMDR is often used in the beginning of treatment to knock down the dopamine response to the addictive substance or behavior. In the DeTUR protocol (Popky, 2005) and the Feeling-State Addiction protocol (Miller, 2012), the client focuses on the triggers to using and how good they feel when they think about doing the substance or the behavior. After rapid eye movements, their urge to use decreases and sometimes disappears. Later, EMDR can be used to clear the trauma that is often underlying addictions.

Ego state therapies may focus on the "addict" part versus the more functional adult part.

Family therapy is a part of many treatment programs and may help provide addicts with a supportive environment while also cleaning up some of the messes that the addiction made.

CIMBS therapy (Sheldon & Sheldon, in press) or other attachment-based therapies can help build a secure base for affect and relationship tolerances, which is lacking in many people who develop addictions.

Trauma therapies. Most people with addictions have a history of trauma. After they have grown some affect tolerance and some sobriety, it becomes possible to use EMDR, ego state therapy, and other trauma therapies to clear the trauma out. When the trauma responses are gone, so are many of the cues to use.

Case History

When he was in his late 30s, John had a great job and a great girlfriend, but he was in big trouble. His addiction to sex with prostitutes threatened his relationship and his solvency (he had more than $80,000 in credit card debt). He was drinking and using marijuana every day. He could not stay off pornography sites. And the supportive psychodynamic therapy he'd been in for two years hadn't touched his addiction problems.

John's history included being raised by a narcissistic, verbally abusive mom and a passive father. When he was ten, a teenage neighbor boy molested him repeatedly. John started using alcohol in his teens and said he didn't finish college due to his binge drinking. He worked in a skilled job that reflected his value of helping people. Two years before we began our work, he'd had a bad breakup, partially over his rages while drinking. He started using porn obsessively, which led to prostitution websites (they're tied together online), and was using and paying for up to five prostitutes each week. In the meantime, he'd met a lovely, sane woman and was in a relationship.

These were John's therapy goals:

1. Stop using porn and prostitution, alcohol, and marijuana.
2. Be able to be present and engaged with what is in front of him.
3. Deal with lifelong shame: "It's not okay to feel good about myself, I've got to be a fuck-up."
4. Deal with PTSD from family (I didn't know about the sexual abuse, so that went on the list later) and PTSD from work.
5. Feel happier.
6. Be more vulnerable with friends and in his relationship.

Therapy techniques:

1. CIMBS for relationship and attachment building
2. EMDR for addiction, trauma, and practicing the future
3. Mindfulness exercises in and out of session
4. Inpatient alcohol and sex addiction therapy
5. Sex and Love Anonymous
6. Coaching on how to get through the hard days
7. Rejoicing when things worked out

Two months into therapy, John had cut his prostitution use from several times a week to every few weeks and was barely drinking. At that time, his girlfriend looked at his phone and found the correspondence with the prostitution sites, and we had an emergency joint session. At that session, she agreed to stay with him, for now, if he went into inpatient treatment. A week later, he flew out of state to spend several weeks as an inpatient at a twelve-step, DBT-oriented treatment center. When he came back, she broke up with him. He remained in AA and Sex and Love Anonymous (SLA) meetings. For a while, therapy centered on feeling the grief and shame of losing the girlfriend while staying abstinent (an SLA requirement).

When the distress cleared, we went back to clearing trauma, and John told me about the sex abuse experience. We cleared that, and much of his shame lifted. So did much of his compulsive sex drive. When we did more work on early attachment and trauma issues with mom, even more of the shame and drive to use porn or to drink went down. During this time, John left the twelve-step programs, saying that they didn't speak to his reasons for using and were too rigid. We both think they had helped him get through the early part of recovery and that he had changed enough to go on without them.

After eighteen months of therapy, treatment, and the twelve-step programs, John was doing much better. He was not using prostitutes and was able to see that he had been exploiting women who, like him, were mostly sexually abused, and he had worked through that guilt. He rarely looked at porn. Instead, when he felt like looking at porn, he would ask himself, "What is it that I'm avoiding?" and stop to feel the avoided affect, breathing through it and talking himself through until it settled. He had been off alcohol since the beginning of treatment, but still used marijuana (a bone of contention in therapy, for sure!). Over the next several months, he came in every two to four weeks for "tune-ups" until he said he was "good to go." Months later, when I called him to ask if I could write his story, he informed me that he'd been "off pot" for several weeks, was dating, was still off porn, and was back to reading books, and was feeling "really good." I told him this news made me happy, and he told me that I had been instrumental in making him happy.

John's story is similar to many in his history of

- attachment breaches and trauma,
- multiple addictions,
- slips and slides on his way to healing,
- many modalities in use to get him "clean,"
- the bad effects of his addictions on his relationships,
- denial of the harm he caused,
- as well as the necessity of healing the trauma and attachment issues before he could be comfortably abstinent.

John was lucky in that he kept his job, had good insurance that covered therapy and treatment centers, and didn't die from his addictions.

Specific Addictions

Eating Disorders

Everyone needs to eat, so abstinence is never a recovery option, which complicates the treatment of all food-based disorders. Eating disorders run from simple addictions to food when stressed or avoidant, to complex interactions of obsessive thinking about body shape, obsessive exercising, and an addiction to the dopamine and endogenous opioids associated with both bingeing and vomiting (purging).

Simple bingeing is the easiest to treat, which doesn't mean it's easy to treat. People may have been substituting food for the love, safety, and soothing they have needed since babyhood. They may have a history of hunger and a reflex to binge when food is available. Or they may have started bingeing to soothe the effects of PTSD. With bingeing, first you get your clients on a regular eating regimen (three meals and one or two healthy snacks a day) of good, protein-rich foods so that they're never horribly hungry. You work on their triggers to bingeing and on their addictions to their chosen binge foods. You increase their affect tolerance with mindfulness and other means. You clear underlying trauma. And you support clients to notice the affect and needs for which they've been substituting food. Depending on the client and the client's history, this may take weeks or months.

With OCD-based obsessions with body-shape and restricted intake, you must go directly to the underlying anxiety. This isn't easy and often takes groups or even inpatient treatment before the client agrees their thinking is indeed "stinking thinking." Here's the gist: *"Every time you notice you're thinking that your 88-pound body is too big, you've got to tell your brain that it's lying to you again and notice the body anxiety that's running that thought. Then you're going to use all the calm-down techniques that we practiced. Imagine doing that right now. And every time you want to avoid that meal in front of you, you've got to stop, notice the anxiety in your body, and remember that starving won't fix the anxiety problem."* These therapies take a long time, often years, to break the shame- and-anxiety-based starving. Get expert consultation when working with this sometimes-fatal condition.

Bingeing and Purging

People caught in the binge–purge cycle have two addictions: one is to the dopamine that comes with eating, and the other is to the strong affect and more dopamine that arises during purging. Vomiting may feel incredibly good, both in meaning (getting rid of that "bad" food and that "bad" action of eating) and in actual physical terms (the dopamine and other chemicals that go with vomiting). These clients can do horrible damage to their throats, mouths, and teeth with the stomach acid they continually bring up. And they often need much more than weekly out-patient treatment. The therapies for this binge-purge disorders include mindfulness, OCD-type thought stopping, then body calming, and then attention to the earlier trauma and attachment issues that underlie most eating disorders. Here, too, get good training and consultation when working with these people!

Internet Addictions

We've had the internet for under thirty years. We've had smart phones with good internet access for about half that. In that time, many of us have become enamored of, then hooked on checking email, news, and posts. Others have found apps, designed to be addictive, to supply us with just enough dopamine—via almost constant wins—to keep us "in the game." For many of us, online life feels as necessary as food. And like most addictions, it's become a tool of avoidance, dysfunctional affect regulation.

How do we know if a client has a problem with online life? How do we help our clients learn to regulate their internet use? Ask. *"Do you ever feel that you spend too much time on the internet? Do you ever use it to avoid other things you need to do? How does playing that game/looking at porn/being on Facebook or Instagram/constantly checking for messages feel? What's great about it?* (Common responses: accessibility, connection, joy of winning, getting off.) *What's not working for you?* (Common responses: wasting time, not getting stuff done, not being around flesh and blood people.) *What would be optimal?* (Common responses: set times to be on and offline, more real-world activities, deleting certain apps.) *How can we work with that?* (As is true for other addictions, we increase affect tolerance with mindfulness and other work; get them to use online time as reinforcement for completing real-world tasks; use the Level of Urge to Avoid protocol (Knipe, 2005) to knock out the dopamine response [if we do EMDR]; and help them make a clear plan to get where they want to go.) I've found it helpful to explain how the various companies are trying to "hook" users. Many clients have used their resentment at the companies to back off of their most addiction-driven online behaviors.

Conclusion

Treating addiction is a tricky business. Addiction is embedded so deeply in people's brains that it can make them go against their good sense, their moral core, and the truth. Expect your clients to lie to themselves and to you about their usage. Expect them to lapse into using their substance or behavior-of-choice many times during the original round of therapy and months or years later. And keep supporting the healthy, life-oriented, willing-to-feel and do-what-it-takes people apart from the addiction. Enjoy the part of this work that is seeing the client set back on their good life track again.

15 / **Treating Depression**

Depression is profoundly physical. It affects cognition, emotion, and nearly every system in the body. When people are depressed, they feel fatigued, sometimes to the point of immobility. They eat and/or sleep too much or not enough. In an attempt to raise their moods, they may consume more sugars, carbohydrates, fats, caffeine, alcohol, or nicotine than they did in their pre-depression lives. Their moods can swing from sadness to extreme irritation and from anxiety to hopelessness to flat inertia. Their cognitions can run from "I suck" (shame) to "the world sucks and always will" (hopelessness). People with depression report anhedonia (loss of pleasure in ordinarily pleasurable activities) and often forget that there ever was pleasure, connection, and meaning in their lives. They are likely to contemplate suicide and are likely to carry it out. Their bodies may hurt, may develop heart disease or diabetes, and may be vulnerable to microbial attacks.

According to centuries of experts, depression is caused by:

- Too much black bile (Hippocrates of Cos, ca. 460–380 BCE); the cure: bloodletting

- An invasion or possession by a nasty spirit (numerous cultures over the last 10,000 years)
- A response of the mind and body to learned helplessness, resulting from being unable to act efficaciously (Seligman, 1991)
- Repression of any motion, notion, or emotion (T. Negri, 1981)
- A chemical imbalance—often too little serotonin dopamine, or another neurotransmitter (medicine); or a lack of the building blocks of serotonin, dopamine, and other neurotransmitters (naturopathy)
- Not enough light stimulating the pineal gland at the right time or, relatedly, a lack of Vitamin D
- Lack of social engagement (Porges, 2005)
- Bad thoughts that cause bad feelings (Burns, 1992)
- Attachment injury causing extreme shame (Knipe, 2008) or "hunkering down" (Shapiro, 2008)
- A bodily response to the triggering of an ego state (van der Hart et al., 2007)
- A disturbance in the homeostasis of the body, originating in the peripheral nervous system, with too much "braking" coming from the parasympathetic side.
- A dorsal vagal response that slows or shuts down many bodily and/ or brain functions to conserve energy, often in response to hyperarousal of an unmyelinated ventral vagal reaction to trauma, emotional or physical stress, or anxiety (Porges, 2017).

Successful treatment for depression helps clients stop unnecessary "braking," be able to "accelerate" at a functional pace, and be capable of social engagement, enjoyment, function, and normal responsive moods (Shapiro, 2009, pp. 9–10). It's helpful to take a multimodal approach to depression, using many of these lenses as a way to understand each client's distress and to find a way to shift them to a new, healthy equilibrium.

Of the many lenses through which one can view depression, the polyvagal theory is an umbrella under which the others fall. It's a simple, comprehensive, well-researched explanation for a complex phenomenon.

And it's easy for me to choose interventions when I look through its lens. Here is polyvagal theory in a nutshell:

The vagus nerve is a huge, three-part nerve that runs through the brain and body. Engagement of the ventral vagus part of the nerve turns us "on." When the evolutionarily older unmyelinated part of the ventral vagus is engaged, we are in a state of high alert. It is often "on" in response to threat or perceived threat. The "newer" myelinated part, the ventral vagus is a mammalian/human innovation. This part is "on" when we are socially or intellectually engaged. It produces a state of pleasant, not overwhelming arousal that seems to be tied to the "affect of interest" and definitely is tied (according to numerous research studies) to social engagement in infants, children, and adults. The phylogenetically oldest part of the nerve, the dorsal vagus, damps down the nervous system and is tied to recuperative states (think of the last time you had a 104-degree temperature), shock, submission, and playing dead. Depression is its chronic manifestation. At our best, we experience constant shifting between the turning on (ventral vagal) and braking (dorsal vagal) mechanisms in our bodies that regulate digestion, heart rate coherence, and many other physical phenomena, including mood and attentiveness. The research on the far-ranging manifestations and implications of the vagal nerve has resulted in new body-based and relational-based treatments for anxiety disorders, major depression, autism, and other disorders (Ogden et al., 2006; Mayo Clinic, 2006; Servan-Schreiber, 2004). When a distressed or a shut-down person becomes truly socially engaged, they shift to a myelinated ventral vagal state with increased heart-rate coherence, engagement of more parts of their thinking brain, and many other effects. (What an elegant explanation for the positive effects of a connected therapeutic relationship!) Some people with formerly intractable depression are being treated with implanted stimulators that supply

> *"Of the many lenses through which one can view depression, the polyvagal theory is an umbrella under which the others fall."*

small electric pulses directly to vagal nerves. In many of these patients, the depressed mood and other symptoms shift appreciably (Mayo Clinic, 2006)

Think about someone with post-traumatic stress disorder. External and internal triggers put them into hyperarousal—afraid and ready to take flight or start a fight. Their amygdala is on fire. Their unmyelinated ventral vagus is on until, after hours, days, months, or years, their body can't handle its red alert status. The dorsal vagal response takes over. The body slows. In some cases, it can barely respond, much less go into an alert state. Their heart rate slows; their digestion shuts down; they just want to sleep or play video games or drink. It's hard for them to connect with others or remember other states (happiness, connectedness, efficacy). Their body, brain, thoughts, and responses are all depressed. They may stay in this shut down state or alternate between hyperarousal (anxiety) and hypoarousal (depression).

Depression seems to coincide with the turning on of the dorsal vagus part of the nerve that suppresses the ventral vagus, thus inhibiting both watchful, aggressive states (unmyelinated) and socially engaged, learning states (myelinated). It has many causes, from strictly biochemical (such as lack of light and nutrients) and/or genetic (as in bipolar and unipolar disorders) to strictly response to a trauma or physical or emotional stress or loss or a response to (often small "t") attachment injuries that caused an inhibition of social engagement (a myelinated ventral vagal function), causing a dorsal vagal reaction. Of course, many depressions have more than one etiology. Chronic depression, whatever the original etiology, can stem from many overlapping causes. And chronic or repeated depression can forge broad neural pathways to cognitive and physical states with millions of connections, making them even harder to transform.

In treating depression, you can utilize many techniques to "flip" the vagal switch. Your clients can start with easy physical interventions: exercise, get more light during winter, and take omega-3 supplements. If there are big "T" traumas, or big "T" or small "t" attachment disruptions, we can clear them with good trauma therapies. Some clients need medication to shift their hormonal balance, stabilize their moods, or change their serotonin levels.

Trauma Therapy for Depression

If a client's depression is clearly trauma-based, EMDR can clear the trauma and the depression will go away. Bessel van der Kolk and his colleagues (2007) did a groundbreaking study comparing the effects of EMDR treatment to Prozac and placebo in traumatized, depressed people. Here's what they found:

> Eighty-eight PTSD subjects diagnosed according to DSM-IV criteria were randomly assigned to EMDR, fluoxetine, or pill placebo. They received 8 weeks of treatment and were assessed by blind raters posttreatment and at 6-month follow-up. The primary outcome measure was the Clinician-Administered PTSD Scale, DSM-IV version, and the secondary outcome measure was the Beck Depression Inventory-II. The study ran from July 2000 through July 2003. (van der Kolk et al., 2007, pp. 11–13)

Here are the results: In only eight sessions of the purest "on-protocol" EMDR, 75% of adult-onset trauma survivors were freed of PTSD and depression. Many of the EMDR group continued to test better on each follow-up test, despite no additional therapeutic intervention. The clinicians in the study found that they cleared the symptoms of most of the child-onset trauma group when they had up to 20 sessions. Clearly, EMDR can clear trauma-based depression.

Some trauma is distinct and easily recounted. Attachment difficulties tied to overt abuse and neglect are easy to spot and easy to target, though not always quick to clear. Some trauma is subtle. Many attachment traumas are repetitive small "t" traumas, for instance, turning away of mother's head when her baby tries to engage her; a rewarding response when the child takes care of mother, forsaking themself; or hunkering down in response to chronically, but vaguely, threatening situations or subtle shaming.

Client History

To treat depression, you need to know its etiology, which may be different in each client. Unless you are faced with the (nearly mythical) perfectly attached, well-supported, low trauma client with one discrete distressing incident and depression ever since, it may take you a while to understand your client's depression and its antecedents. I do most intakes using Maureen Kitchur's Strategic Developmental Model (SDM; 2005). The SDM is anchored by a genogram (family tree) and an extensive client and family history. Among its nosy, snoopy questions are queries about depression, alcoholism, and other disorders in the family. I usually highlight the representations of depressed family members on the family tree with a colored marking pen. If there is a family history of depression, it becomes graphically obvious to both my client and me. Clients often say something like, "Oh, it's not just me!" The intake procedure, especially the genogram, can give them a context for their malady.

It's not enough to determine the presence of familial depression. Keep asking questions that explain the context of depression in the family. If there are four generations of bipolar disorder, the diagnosis may seem straightforward. But keep in mind that your client's depression may arise from the big "T" and small "t" traumas of being parented by an impaired caregiver, not her genetics. A family of Holocaust survivors may hand down nongenetic depression from the effects of generational trauma (Shapiro, 2005a). Here are some other questions to ask your clients, whether or not there is a family history of depression:

- *What kind of parent was your mother's mother? Her father? Your father's parents?*
- Note the disruptions of attachment that can come with premature

birth, illness, military service, birth of other children, and separations. *Were your parents or siblings hospitalized when you were young? Were you? Were either of your parents gone from home for more than a few days? Were you?*

- What stressors faced the parents and grandparents? Were they broke? Immigrants from a war-torn country? Living in a dangerous neighborhood? Soldiers? Living in a rigid, unforgiving community?
- *What kinds of abuse happened in each generation?*
- *Who used alcohol or drugs? Any alcoholics/addicts?*
- *Who has been to therapy? Do you know why?*
- *Do you know if anyone in your family is taking antidepressants? Other psychotropic medications/drugs?*
- *Has anybody been hospitalized for depression? Other emotional reasons?*
- *What kinds of illnesses run in your family?*
- *What is your health history?*

"It's not enough to determine the presence of familial depression. Keep asking questions that explain the context of depression in the family."

This last question is extremely important in diagnosing depression. Joseph McCreery, a Seattle psychiatrist, allowed me to print his good advice on my blog, www.traumatherapy.typepad.com (2007):

> "Any moderately or severely depressed, anxious or chronically fatigued patient should have a medical lab screen (if not obtained within the last year) to include: complete blood count, thyroid functions, and a chemistry panel including electrolytes, BUN, creatinine and liver function tests. Sleep apnea is another physical disorder that contributes to fatigue, depression, anxiety (and increased risk of cardiovascular problems). Any patient with snoring, periods of about 10 seconds of apnea (no breathing)

followed by a deep snoring or snorting inhalation and accompanied by day time sleepiness should be sent for a sleep evaluation. Medical abnormalities such as these, when screened for and treated, can do much to improve patients' well-being and improve therapy outcomes. These tests can easily be done by a primary care provider at a therapist's request. (personal communication)

I've sent depressed clients to physicians who have found thyroid dysregulation, chronic fatigue syndrome, or blood pressure problems. When the physical problems were treated, the depressive symptoms went away.

Assessing Depression

After you've learned their histories, you need to know your client's present situation.

- What do they do? What do they like/hate about their job/school/household/status?
- What kind of social connections do they have? (Isolation is depressing, and depression causes isolation.)
- What are their current life stressors? Ask about finances, relationships, family, roommates, commute, etc.
- What are their current joys, interests, obsessions?
- Are there any recent losses of people, pets, or status? Are there any changes? Moves? Job changes? Graduation?

Once you have the context of their lives, you can zero in on the symptoms of their depression. You may buy Beck's famous, often-revised inventory of 21 questions (Beck, Ward, Mendelson, Mock, & Erbaugh, 1961). You also can download the ten-question MDI, Major Depression Inventory, from the World Health Organization (http://www.who-5.org/). Or you can embed your questions in your intake, leaving room for explanations and digressions.

You might start with the following questions and use your clinical curiosity and your heartfelt human response to follow up on each answer:

- *How long have you felt like this?*
- *Did something in particular happen to bring it on?*
- *Does it come and go, or is it constant?*
- *What do you feel like inside when you're depressed? How bad is it right now?*
- *What other physical symptoms do you have?*
- *How is your sleep? Too much? Not enough? Any early waking?*
- *How is your eating? Do you have an appetite? Are you craving sugar and caffeine? Are you eating too much? Bingeing? Tell me about it.*
- *What's your concentration like? Do you have trouble reading? Paying attention?*
- *Are you tired much of the time? Tell me more.*
- *How is your motivation to get things done?*
- *Are you avoiding doing what you need to do? How badly are you beating yourself up for that?*
- *Some people get isolated when they feel low. What's happening in your social life?*
- *Some people get low when they are isolated. What kind of relationships do you have?*
- *What's your enjoyment level? Can you remember enjoying things more before this depression grabbed you? Do you have any sex drive? Do you still like food? Is there anything that still gives you joy?*
- *Do you get nervous? What's that like? Do you have worried thoughts over and over?*
- *Are you feeling guilty a lot of the time? Are you blaming yourself for things you really aren't in control of?*

- *Do you feel irritable a lot of the time? How is your patience?*
- *What are you doing to avoid this depression? Drinking? Eating? Gambling? Overworking?*
- *Do you have any feelings of hopelessness?* (With some younger clients I ask: *Does everything suck? Do you suck? Do you think you or it will always suck?*)
- *Do you ever feel that life isn't worth it?*
- *Are you having any suicidal thoughts? How strong are they? Any plans? What keeps you alive? What do you think could push you over the edge? Is it that you want to be dead or that you want this bad feeling to stop?*

The answers to these questions will give you a rough idea of your client's experience. The next step is to decide on your plan of attack.

Treatment Planning

Sometimes it's easy. You spot the symptoms of low thyroid function (hair loss, fatigue, weight gain, and cold hands and feet), send them to their doctor or an endocrinologist, and do supportive therapy until the drugs kick in and the patient feels back to normal. Or, you notice that depression kicked in a month after last year's car accident, and you clear the trauma with EMDR or other trauma therapy, and your grateful and newly buoyant client smiles as they wave goodbye. Or, spotting the family history of bipolar disorder/postpartum depression/major depression and seeing all the symptoms in your client, you send them to a psychiatrist or ARNP (advanced registered nurse practitioner) for medication (and they actually go and actually take their medication), and they follow your self-care suggestions.

Other cases are more complex, harder to figure out, and/or take longer to resolve. While continuing to explore the cause of the depressed state (sending the client to your most savvy diagnostician and/or asking more questions) you can move ahead with interventions that help most depressed people, whatever the etiology of their depression. Nearly any kind of regular exercise, omega-3 (fish oil) supplements, guided exercises that increase heart rate coherence, and social engagement all help raise one's mood from the depths (Servan-Schreiber, 2004). If a client is immobilized by depression, medical intervention will be your first step. If they have enough mobilization to allow their friends to drag them out for a daily walk, get to the store for fish oil, and come connect with you, you might see improvement in the first few weeks.

It's helpful to explain what's happening in physical terms. I find that this is less shaming than other explanations. *"Your body has a three-part nerve that connects to your brain. One part turns on to put you in red alert, fight or flight mode. One part turns on when you're socially or pleasantly engaged.*

> **"Clients need to know that you are joined with them against their symptoms."**

And one is the dimmer switch, slowing down body and brain responses. It sounds like your dimmer switch has been stuck on low for a long time, causing your depression. We're going to work together to turn the light back on."

You can add whatever further explanation makes sense:

- *After that surgery/long illness/stressful time at work/getting through the divorce, your body turned down the dimmer switch to force you to rest. We've got some work to do to get your energy turned back on.*
- *Your whole life, you've been using that dimmer switch to turn off your true self to try to please the people around you. You haven't done it on purpose; it's a reflex that happened in childhood and then automatically kept going. Your official diagnosis is* depression. *Our working diagnosis is* hunkered down *and our treatment plan is to "un-hunker" you to turn that energy switch back on.* (I've had several clients say

words to the effect of "You really get me!" after this explanation of their diagnosis.)

- *When we did your family tree, we saw how depression has colonized your mother's family. Some of what you're experiencing is the effect of having a depressed mom. When she couldn't respond to you when you were a baby, your dimmer switch went on and stayed partially on for much of your life. We can clear that part of your depression with therapy. It seems that you may have inherited some of the physically based depression and anxiety, too. We're going to work on some management skills to help you turn down both the dimmer switch and the mobilization/anxiety switch so that you can feel more balanced. If we can't turn down the switch quickly, I want you to meet with my nurse practitioner/psychiatrist colleague, who may prescribe some medications that can get you up and functioning so that our other therapies have a chance to work.*

Notice that I used "we" in each example. Depression is daunting. Clients need to know that you are joined with them against their symptoms. Be transparent about what you think is the cause. If you can't figure it out, you can say so and keep looking for the causes. Use general practitioners, neurologists, psychiatrists, and your most invasive curiosity until the symptoms make sense to you and your client. In the meantime, use your best management skills to help them deal with their symptoms. I've run into four cases that made no sense to me. It turned out that two were based in head injuries, that hadn't turned up in the intake. Now I always ask, *"Did you ever get hit in the head or fall on your head?"* in my nosy, snoopy intake. Another woman had a rare metabolic disorder that lowers dopamine, exacerbated by a constant bombarded of neurotoxins from her mold-infested rental house. She became less dopey and more focused when she got out of the moldy house. It took an internist, a psychiatric nurse practitioner, and me two years of befuddlement before we understood the clinical picture." (Shapiro, 2009, pp. 13–19)

Treating Depression

If you know the etiology, go after it. There are no known genetic markers for depression, per se. However, people prone to anxiety may have more inflammation and get less inflammation-reducing sleep. Inflammation creates cytokines that float through the body and induce lethargy and a dorsal vagal state. (Think about having a fever knocking you out.) Treat the anxiety, and the depression often lightens.

Bipolar disorder is a disease of mania. In the manic state, some people have higher anxiety; some people don't sleep much or at all; some people run around manically. The cytokines come in, knock bring in the dorsal state, and you've got depression. Treat the mania with medications and mindfulness, and the depression often lifts. If the client has spent years in the up-and-down bipolar cycle, there may be a lot of neural networks dedicated to the depressed state and the manic one. You may have to go into full bore depression recovery to keep them out of that shut-down/reparative state.

Trauma causes inflammation, which causes depression. It also causes shut-down, endogenously created dissociative states in response to the out-of-control affect of PTSD. And in PTSD, the trauma is played over and over, creating more inflammation and possibly more shut-down. Clear the trauma with your best trauma therapy. As the van der Kolk and colleagues (2007) study shows, if you clear the adult-onset trauma, the depression usually goes away (2007). If there is chronic childhood trauma, it may take longer but the same applies. Don't just treat the symptoms! Go after the causes!

Grief

Depression is a normal part of mourning. Normalize it. Help your clients to feel the anger, sadness, and reality of the loss. Generally, even for a huge loss, the client will eventually feel their energy and interest in the world rise, and they will start to feel better. Warn them that grief comes in waves and that the depression part may come and go. There is the progression of grief, which may occur in succession or over and over. Help your clients sit with each stage. Normalize the stages. And ask your client to locate each feeling in their body. Help them notice that the thoughts of each state (e.g., "It's hopeless!") are thoughts tied to deep emotion, and promise them that if they feel those emotions, the feelings will eventually move on.

Stages of Grief

Shock and disbelief: "He can't be gone!"

1. Anger and blaming: Self, the one who is gone, doctors, fate, God, or someone else
2. Sadness, depression, hopelessness, and yearning
3. Integration of each of the above
4. Over the acute grief, but still missing the person or situation that is lost.
   (Adapted from Elizabeth Kubler-Ross's excellent 2005 book, *On Grief and Grieving: Finding the Meaning of Grief Through the Five Stages of Loss.*)

Rules of Grief, for normalizing the experience

Grief always hurts more than you think it should.

1. It always lasts longer then you (and others) think it ought.
2. It makes you feel tired, cranky, stupid, or hopeless.
3. Avoid it, and it stays terrible and creates depression and/or useless busyness.
4. Feel it all, and it gets better. (Shapiro, 2018)

Out-of-Session Strategies

Clients need to combat their depression every day. No matter what the source, these strategies should help:

1. At least 30 minutes of aerobic exercise daily—60 minutes is even better: walk, run, bike, or do some group aerobic activity. Extremely depressed people may need their friends to drag them out of the house for exercise.
2. Consume nutritious food. For severely depressed people, help them get microwavable dinners and other easily prepared nutritious foods into the house and into their diets.
3. If you live in a dark northern climate, have them get a lightbox and take extra vitamin D in the winter.
4. Strongly support your clients to be around other people who like them. For severely depressed people, either have them call friends during the session to make dates for socializing or to take them to a meeting or gathering.
5. Mindfulness or yoga classes are a great idea. It gets people out of their houses, and it teaches them skills that let their mood run through instead of over them.
6. Listening to music and singing along boosts mood. Have them try it, and see if it helps.

Medical Interventions

Find a good psychiatrist, ARNP, or doctor well-versed in treating depression, to work with your client. Make sure that this person is willing to collaborate and communicate with you. There are many medications for depressed bodies that work for many, but not all, people. Transcranial stimulation, neurofeedback, and one-time ketamine injections work for other people. Good practitioners will talk to you and your client about what can work and why.

If you suspect low thyroid or another hormonal problem, send your client directly to a specialist. A 30-year-old man came into my practice complaining of deep depression. He had an extremely low sex drive and unusually soft-looking features. I sent him to an endocrinologist who diagnosed him with low testosterone, found a nonmalignant tumor that they removed, and solved the "depression" problem within a week of implementing a testosterone supplement. And I have sent many thyroid-deficient clients to endocrinologists who "cured" them of depression in weeks.

Chronic Depression

There can be many, often overlapping, causes of chronic depression.

1. Early attachment experience: When babies are not responded to with joy and adoration, they don't develop a strong neural network for joy. They also don't know that they're "good." These kids live with shame and an inability to live in joy. Parents who are grieving, depressed, or had their own poor attachments can't give their kids the experiences to develop the neural networks for joy and robust, depression-proof psyches. This underlying cause calls for longer, attachment-based therapy which includes provoking and acknowledging the joy of human connection.

2. Trauma: Untreated trauma, replaying over and over, causes the inflammatory response that underlies many cases of depression. Clear it!

3. Illness or chemical imbalance: Skilled medical intervention is necessary.

4. Multiple or enormous losses: People who've lost children, a spouse, a treasured job/meaningful activity, a sense of safety, or a community may be depressed for a long time. A child who loses a parent and has no other love/support person may fall into deep depression. Help these people grieve. Encourage them to feel it all. Then, as the grief slowly moves

through, encourage them to begin to connect with other people, places, and/or meaning of living after the loss.

Don't lose hope with these clients. Therapy is helpful, and it may take a long time to develop the neural networks of joy and connection and freedom from shame. Get support for yourself if you start to catch your client's hopelessness.

Shame-Based Depression

Damasio (1999) said that what we know about ourselves is based largely about what feels true. Shame is profoundly visceral and intellectual: "I'm bad." It comes from the inhibitory response that children have when their behavior is either punished or completely ignored. Chronically depressed people are often programmed for hunkered-down self-hatred. Any attempt to reason or argue with them about it is responded to with incomprehension. "I just know that I'm bad. I've always been bad. Just because you like me or think I'm not a jerk, doesn't change anything." It often comes down to preverbal experiences.

Jim Knipe (2008) says

> "The formation of a core identity is one of the tasks of childhood. This task can go awry in many ways for a child living in a dysfunctional environment. For such children, it's logical to say that, 'It is better to be a bad child with good parents than a good child with bad parents.' It seems true, both intuitively and from clinical practice, that for an abused child, a sense of 'badness' about self may be less horrible than an awareness of the full reality and implications of abuse—the shock, the betrayal, the confusion, the vulnerability of being little in a world of uncaring big adults. If you are a 'bad' child with good parents, you still have good parents, at least in your mind. You then have hope, because

you could someday learn to be a perfect child, and maybe your parents would finally give you the love, acceptance and guidance you need. Of course, there are many possible reasons why parents might be 'bad' or deficient in their caretaking role—illness, their own mental disturbance, fear of parenting responsibilities, narcissism, addictions—to name a few. Parents who are frightened or immature will often project their own doubts and fears onto their children with shaming words (e.g., 'You are a crybaby,' 'You are a brat,' 'What's wrong with you!!? You are too . . . noisy, angry, needy, quiet, anxious,' etc.). Whatever the cause, for many children attempting to make sense of a dysfunctional family situation, a self-definition of "badness" is an adaptive and compelling option. We could use psychodynamic language and say that the identity of shame serves as a psychological defense, protecting the child in such circumstances from the full impact of traumatic loss and emotional abandonment."

Knipe continues "For these clients, the traumatic origins of their shame feelings were dissociated and not available to the adult ego state. Consequently, each client experienced a self-definition of profound defectiveness and moral badness. This negative identity was driven by both sensory information (a feeling of shamefulness) and intellectual conviction. Body sensations are a major determinant of the sense of knowing what is real, what is true, what is happening, or what has happened in the past. Thus, for each of the cases described here, comprehensive therapy involved processing negative identity and self-referencing negative cognitions (NCs), and specific and detailed focus on the deeply entrenched feelings and sensations that were intrinsic parts of shamefulness."

Knipe has a delightful way of working with these issues. He is an EMDR therapist who uses bilateral stimulation with ego state intervention. If you don't use EMDR, you can still do the ego state part to good avail. Here is my quick-and-dirty version of his protocol:

1. *Can you connect with the adult part of you, the part that goes to work and takes care of the kids and is right here and now with me?*

2. *Let me explain shame to you. Little kids push themselves down to keep from doing things that either get a bad reaction from parents or cause them to be ignored. Kids who were abused, like you were, try to push down the "cause," which feels like their inherent badness. Because why else would they get abused or ignored? It must be their fault.*

3. *Let me ask you a question: Do you think that every child on this planet deserves to be treated with kindness and to be protected from abuse and to be loved by the adults around them?*

4. *Good. Keep that in mind, because your internal kid's shame might try to shift that.*

5. *Right now, I want this adult part of you to go back in time and find that little one that you were, who was treated so badly/ignored/not seen/criticized all the time.*

6. *Bring that little one all the way up here, and put that child in the kid-sized chair that's appeared right next to you.*

7. *Imagine a big-screen tv shows up in front of you both. And both of you watch a brief movie of that abuse/criticism/etc. that happened in this kid's life.*

8. *What does the kid see when they watch? And who do they blame for what happened? And why are they to blame? Because the kid is bad.*

9. *Back to the adult you, who knows why a child would say that it was their fault. What do you, as an adult, see in that scene? Does any child have the power to make adults act that way? You think so? So, if it were me who got abused that way, would you say that about me? No? So back up a bit, and look again. Would any child be responsible for having a mother/father like that? No? So, what do you see now?*

10. *Now that you're sure that this child is blameless, turn this child around to face you. Look at this child with loving eyes. Tell the child they didn't control those parents. Tell this child that they were just a baby/little child and that those parents/adults were that way before*

they ever had a child. That they were born into a family where the people could hurt even the best kids. Tell that little one that they are with you now and that you know that they are a good kid and never, ever, deserved to be treated that way. That they deserve love, care, and protection. That they deserved to be adored! Can you look at this child with the same adoring eyes you give your offspring? Good! Do it! Let this child get used to feeling that loving connection that they always deserved.

11. *Now every time the shame feeling comes up, we're going to go back to that kid, and bring them up here again to learn what you and I know: that they are a good kid. That they deserved care, protection, and adoration. And that they live right here and now, in this year, with you and occasionally me. And that we both know that they're loveable.*

Conclusion

Depression strikes many clients from many directions. No matter how your clients became depressed, stress that they are not to blame for their profoundly physical disease. Connect with them. Support them. And work every angle you know to change their dorsal vagal depressed state to a connected and lively one.

16 / **Sexual Issues**

Until you get used to it, sex can be difficult to discuss with clients. However, if you treat it like any other topic, your clients will, too. Use normal language. Don't shy away from the content.

Healthy sexuality includes the ability to be aroused, connect with another person, stay present during sex, say "no" when something is not working, give direction on what can work better, and to have orgasms, fun, and connection in the process.

Here are some of the sexual issues that may show up in therapy and some ways to help:

- Worries about attractiveness or function:
  - Find out whether the problem is simply anxiety or the person has functional problems. If it's a functional problem you can ask, *"What happens when you masturbate? Can you bring yourself to orgasm? Can you tell another person how to help you get there?"* If it's not a functional problem, work with their anxiety as you would with any anxiety: calm-down techniques, mindfulness, and imagining talking with another person or walking through the sexual situation.

- If it's a functional issue, instruction is in order. Suggest the squeeze technique for premature ejaculation or recommend methods from the amazing website www.OMGyes.com for instructing both men and women how to bring women to orgasm. (Check it out, but don't watch videos from it in session with your clients. It's quite graphic.)

- A history of childhood sexual abuse or assault, resulting in avoiding sex, or having flashbacks or becoming dissociated during sexual encounters:
  - No sex until they can show up for it!
  - Go after the trauma memories with your best trauma therapy until they're out of that person's body and mind.
  - If the person was abused by a man, the most likely perpetrator, try this: *"When you think of being abused, can you feel his penis inside of you? His hands on you? Do you want to pull his hands, his penis, and his tongue out of your body, forever? Let's get rid of it! Imagine putting on your sterile gloves. A hole has just opened at your feet that goes to the center of the Earth. Now, reach towards the places that hold his body parts in you, and pull out all of him. Keep pulling them out. Keep pulling until they're all gone. Keep going. . . Are they all out? What would you like there instead? Fill up with YOU! Fill up with healing! Great! How does that feel, now?"*
  - You can use the Two-Hand technique to differentiate their current partner from the abuser: *"In one hand, hold that guy who molested/raped you. In the other, hold that nice man you married. How close to each other do those hands feel? Where should they be? Good, separate them. Hold them even further apart. Now think about your sweet husband, can you say 'no' to him? Can you ask him to stop doing something that's uncomfortable? Did you have that ability with the person who raped you?"* Or *"When you were a little girl getting raped by that guy, how big were you? Think of your body now. Put the little girl's body and ability to protect*

herself in one hand. Put your grown-up sexual body in the other. Which one is safer? Which one wants to have sex with her chosen partner? Tell that little girl that it's illegal for her to be in a sexual situation, so she needs to stay out of your bed when you want to have grown-up married sex."

- Being part of a generation that dates, marries, and connects sexually less frequently than any other living generation: Access to sexual partners is a huge problem for people in their twenties and thirties. You will need to do a lot of coaching to get some of your clients through the online dating rabbit hole, and to help them know that they're not alone in their frustration.

- Not knowing how to do it: Porn is a horrible way to learn, since those people are actors. Tell all clients to read books, watch instruction sites, and refer to www.OMGyes.com for pleasuring women, and work with them—especially women—on saying "No"; saying "Could you do it this way?"; and explaining exactly what works.

- Addiction to pornography (usually men): This habit or addiction can lead to unrealistic expectations of oneself and one's partners and lead one away from good relationships. (Read Chapter 14, Treating Addiction, for a case history.)

- Not being able to say no or ask for needs to be met (usually women): Do lots of work with the parts that don't know what they want or how to ask.

- Confusion about sexuality or gender: In general, there are three spectrums with these issues
  - *Sexual orientation:* Who am I attracted to? People can be completely heterosexual, completely homosexual, or anything in between. During a lifetime, people may shift a little one way or the other, but rarely does anyone jump from one end of the spectrum to the other. Your job is to support the exploration, note the societal expectations, and support the client wherever they are. Sexual orientation is an innate brain thing and is not

subject to change by psychotherapy. If a client easily comes out to you, you might ask a few questions, like *"How long have you been out?"* or *"Are you in a relationship?"* or *"Are you connected to a community?"* If they are struggling with the issue, be there with them, and let them know that you're in their corner, whoever or whatever they are. Other questions might include

- *When did you first notice you were attracted to men/women/ all genders?*
- *What did you feel about it then? How about now?*
- *Have you talked to people about it?*
- *What kind of response did you/do you fear you will get?*
  It's helpful for newly coming out or conflicted people to meet other people in their situation via in person or online support groups. All big cities have these groups; otherwise online is the way to go.

- *How masculine or feminine does my culture think I am?* Few of us fit the criteria for 100% masculine or 100% feminine. Most of us lean one way or the other, regardless of sexual orientation. Some people question their sexuality, when really, the issue is our society's rigid definition of gender roles. Help these people see where they fit in, regardless of who they think is cute and whatever body they think they should have.

- *Am I male or female?* This speaks to brain structure. What plumbing we're born with may not fit the gender of our brains. Strongly support your clients to hang out in not knowing until they know. Support groups, especially in-person ones, can be very helpful for people with this dilemma. And for people who know for sure, support them where they are and help them deal with the cultural hell of their "differentness".

- Cultural Issues: All human issues are situated in culture. Sex, even more so. Pay careful attention to your client's background. Ask about how sex was discussed, if it was, in their household. Did they belong to a church or community with rigid views of sexual roles and behavior? Many fundamentalist communities of every religion see no sexual role for women, except as always-available recipients of their husbands' attention. In some families, the discussion of sex was shameful and forbidden. In other households, there was constant talk of sex, attractiveness, and fantasy. You may need to expand the client's contexts of appropriate and legitimate sexuality.

Sex Therapy Goals

Important goals include the ability: to choose when and when not to have sex, to be aroused, to connect with another person, to stay present during sex, to say "no" when something is not working, to give direction on what can work better, and to have orgasms, fun, and connection. Differentiation is a necessary component of good sex. Renowned sex therapist David Schnarch (1991) says that differentiation is possible when each partner can love all of themselves, even the parts that the other partner doesn't like; and each partner can love all of the other, even the parts that they don't like very much. Schnarch says that to have good sex, we have to be able to accept our own hungers, our own bodies, and the way our bodies want to be pleasured; and we have to be able to do the same for our partners: see them, accept them, and help them along. Both partners need to "hold onto themselves" to "hold onto each other." You may spend a lot of time in therapy working clients into the differentiated stance of self- and other-acceptance.

17 / **Final Stages**

The trauma and shame and depression are cleared. Your client has more tolerance for a range of affect, is functioning better, is out in the world, and is feeling more content and even happy. What do you do now?

What's Next?

Clients who previously had good function, goals, social connection, and meaning can go right back to their preproblem lives. Clients who didn't have those things need to make plans.

You're doing wonderfully. Now that you have your energy back and you're able to connect to people so much better, what else do you want in your life?

1. *Got any goals? Anything that you've seen other people do or that they have that looks good to you? Go inside, and see if there's a wish that you'd like to fulfill. What are the steps to getting there?*
2. *You've got an advanced degree, and through all those years of depression, you've hated your low-level job. Is it time for you to move up to*

a job you love, or at least can stand? What's your criteria for the new job? What are the steps to getting that job?

3. *You want a relationship! Now that you've cleared so much family trauma, you can pick one that is much more functional than where you came from. What are the criteria you have for a good partner? What qualities does that person have? What must they absolutely not have or be? And what kind of relationship do you want to build?*

4. *Now that you're feeling better and know how to connect, how are you going to start making good social connections? What kinds of people do you want to connect with? What kinds of things do you want to do with them?*

5. *Now that you no longer dissociate, you've got just one consciousness here, all the time. Now that your time isn't split up between parts, you're telling me that you're getting bored. So it's time for you to learn a new skill: entertaining yourself. It's time to try out new ways to fill and kill time. You get to find out what's fun, what's not, and what you like. Let's make a list of possible ways to entertain yourself with and without other people, and see what appeals to you when you think about or try them out.*

6. *We've done a lot together. You're out of that horrible depression. You're out of that shame, and you know that you're a good human. You've got a good job. And you've found a great guy. Are there any other goals that you want to reach in your therapy?*

Final Sessions

If you've seen someone for a few sessions and the trauma work or normalization or advice worked well and they're on their way, there's not much to do but acknowledge the work, acknowledge the relationship, ask if they have anything they need to do or say to be complete, and let them know that you're available for another round, when and if they need it.

If you've had a months or years of therapy together, it's important to acknowledge the work you've done together, your relationship, and that the end of it (or this round) has meaning and emotional consequences. For example:

- *Now that we're at the end, is there anything that you need to say or do to be complete with this process? Is there anything that, six weeks from now, you will be wishing you had said, either something positive or something that didn't work for you here?*
- *We have been with each other a long time and worked through a lot. What's standing out for you, now? . . . And I want to remind you that you've also done _____ and _____ and _____.*
- *What's it going to be like for you to not be seeing me?*
- *I'm grown very attached to you over these months/years together. I'm going to miss you, too.*
- *What are you feeling right now?*
- *I'm planning to be in practice for a long time. If you ever need a refresher, you can call me.*
- *As you know, I'm closing my practice now. Here is a list of people you can call if you ever need another round.*

It's often both exhilarating and sad to say goodbye to a long-term client. It's lovely to review how you and the client cocreated the client's clinical transformation. And your client may be afraid to say goodbye. It's important to discuss the function that regular therapy has had for the client. And to talk about what the client will do without it. If you're planning to be around, you can offer follow-up services. If you're not going to be around, or you're terminating therapy before the client is finished, you can

> **"Acknowledge the work, acknowledge the relationship, ask if they have anything they need to do or say to be complete."**

offer referrals. However, don't do any of these without speaking to your mutual attachment and what the loss of it means and feels like. Make sure you wish your client well and you accept their well wishes. And notice what it feels like not to witness the next chapter of the long story that you've been a part of.

18 / **Self-Care for Therapists**

As therapists, we are privileged to watch our clients' trauma fade from terrible, here-and-now experiences to mere memories, their dissociation shift to integrated presence, and their pain disappear. We get to watch anxious clients become calmer and more able to do whatever they need to do. We get to watch clients release their depression and be able to experience joy, and watch clients become free of their addictions and tolerant of all their emotions.

We are also privy to the gut-wrenching details of rape, accidents, war, and story after story of child abuse, domestic violence, and horrible neglect. The more terrible the abuse and the more dissociated the clients, the more they project the actual emotions of their trauma into us. Some therapists become grim. Some avoid complex trauma clients. Some let their clients avoid expressing affect in the sessions. Some burn out and leave the profession. Some become vicariously traumatized and begin to feel avoidant about particular clients or work in general. Here are some ways to keep yourself whole while doing this important work.

1. Do your own work. If you're not able to tolerate your own history and your current affect, you won't be able to tolerate the despair,

rage, shame, and grief that move through many trauma survivors. Find yourself good therapy until you can be fully present with yourself and your clients.

2. Learn mindfulness. Meditate or do yoga, qigong, or breathing exercises. It will help you "stay in the chair" while witnessing whatever whatever arises. Learn to breathe and ground yourself while being with anything.

3. Know yourself. If you begin a session in a state of equilibrium, and you start feeling rage or exhaustion in the session, guess that it may be the client's rage or dissociation. You may then ask the client, *"What are you feeling right now? There's something in the room."* The client is likely to say, "Oh, I'm angry. I guess it's about _____ or, "Oh, I was just spacing out." When you know where you are, you will know when you are being drawn into someone else's experience and will be able to use it for their benefit.

4. Know the signs of burnout and vicarious traumatization.
   - You aren't excited to go to work.
   - You talk only about work and have no other interests.
   - You treat everyone on Earth like a client.
   - You dream about clients, especially bad dreams.
   - You're angry at clients for being the way they are.
   - You feel shame for your human limitations.
   - You have vicarious trauma reactions: flashbacks, anxiety, depression, or avoidance around client material.
   - You want to drink, gamble, or otherwise dissociate after work.

5. Get support.
   - Join a supportive consultation group. (Not just about a technique, but about you, too. And no shaming allowed.)
   - Get individual consultation for the most troubling cases. As a consultant, I'm going step by step with a few consultees with their most fragile, barely tractable cases. It's good for the therapists and good for the clients.
   - Do your own work. Hire a good trauma therapist who can help

you clear your vicarious trauma. If you have your own trauma history, you must deal with it before your clients trigger your own unhealed wounds.

6. Increase your therapeutic arsenal. If what you're doing isn't working, find something that will. Become a constant learner. The more lenses through which you can see your clients, the more interest and efficacy you'll have. The more effective you are, the less likely you are to burn out.

7. Develop interests that have nothing to do with therapy. Make sure some of them involve unmitigated joy.

8. Do things that bring you into your body: run, stretch, work out, dance, do yoga.

9. If you have any control over your schedule and case load, limit the number of the most complex, dissociated, abused, unstable clients you see. And don't see all of your complex clients on the same day.

10. You will probably learn your tolerance the way most of us do, by exceeding it. Once you know, maintain your own boundaries. Follow the Platinum Rule: "Fill your own cup first; give away only what's left over." Another rule: "To thine own self be nice." Therapy is compelling, but don't let it run your entire life.

11. Watch out for grandiosity. You can't fix everything. Know your limits.

12. Know what's realistic. In the consultation group that I attend, all of us work with complex dissociated clients. It's helpful to see other people's clients inch forward when we all want ours to leap forward.

13. If you have a spiritual practice, use it to support your work. When you're stuck, ask whatever higher power you believe in for help.

Take care of yourself while you enjoy this great profession!

Further Resources

CBT

There are thousands of CBT interventions in hundreds of books, for both clients and therapists. Here are some good ones for practitioners: *Cognitive Behavior Therapy: Basics and Beyond* (2nd ed.) by Beck (2011); *Cognitive Therapy of Depression* by Beck, Rush, Shaw, & Emer (1987); *Mindfulness-Based Cognitive Therapy for Depression* (2nd ed.) by Segal, Williams, Teasdale (2013) and their client-oriented book, *The Mindful Way Workbook* (2014). Other books for clients include *Mind Over Mood: Change How You Feel by Changing the Way You Think* by Greenberger & Padesky (2016) and *Feeling Good* (1992) and *The Feeling Good Handbook* (1999) by David Burns.

DBT

Linehan, M. (1993). *Skills Training Manual for Treating Borderline Personality Disorder*. New York: Guildford Press.

EMDR

There are more than one hundred EMDR books. In order to perform EMDR, you must take an official "EMDRIA-approved" six-day training.

Books that introduce EMDR include:

Shapiro, F. (2017). *Eye Movement Desensitization and Reprocessing*. New York: Guilford Press.

Maiberger, B. (2009). *EMDR Essentials: a guide for clients and therapists*. New York: W. W. Norton & Company.

Books that blend EMDR with other psychotherapies:

Arad, H. (2018). *Integrating Relational Psychoanalysis and EMDR*. New York: Routledge.

Schwartz. A., & Maiberger, B. (2018). *EMDR Therapy and Somatic Psychology*. New York: W. W. Norton & Company.

Books that integrate EMDR with ego state therapies:

Paulsen, S. (2009). *Looking through the Eyes of Trauma and Dissociation*. South Carolina: Booksurge Publishing.

Knipe, J. (2014). *EMDR Toolbox: Theory and Treatment of Complex PTSD and Dissociation*. New York: Springer.

Shapiro, R. (2016). *Easy Ego State Interventions*. New York: W. W. Norton & Company.

Forgash, C., & Copeley, M. (2008). *Healing the Heart of Trauma and Dissociation with EMDR and ego state therapy*. New York: Springer.

Self-help books include:

Parnell, L. (2008*). Tapping In: A Step-by-Step Guide to Activating Your Healing Resources Through Bilaterial Stimulation*. Louisville, Colorado: Sounds True.

Shapiro, F. (2012). *Getting Past your Past: Take control of your life with self-help techniques from EMDR therapy*. New York: Rodale.

Ego State Therapy

Helen Watkins and John Watkins, *Ego States: Theory and Therapy* (1997), is the best and was one of the first.

My book *Easy Ego State Interventions* (2015) is an introduction and practical guide to using these interventions for working with couples issues, trauma, personality disorders, and dissociation.

Forgash and Copeley's *Healing the Heart of Trauma and Dissociation with EMDR and Ego State Therapy* (2008) is a compilation, describing many different ego state therapies and how they are used with EMDR. It's useful, even if you don't yet use EMDR.

Paulsen's *Looking Through the Eyes of Trauma and Dissociation: An Illustrated Guide for EMDR Therapists and Clients* (2009) is a good guide for general parts work, whether or not you do EMDR. It is simple enough for clients to understand.

Hypnotherapy

Training for Hypnotherapy

Stephen Gilligan: https://www.stephengilligan.com/

The American Society of Clinical Hypnosis:https://www.asch.net/Education/
RegionalWorkshops/WorkshopsSchedule.aspx

Books on Hypnotherapy

There are dozens of good hypnotherapy books. Here are some of the best:

Calof, D. (1996). *The Couple Who Became Each Other and Other Tales of Healing
from a Hypnotherapist's Casebook.* New York: Bantam.
A fascinating read by my teacher and consultant of the last 25 years.

Erickson, M., Rossi, E., Rossi, S. (1976). *Hypnotic Realities: The Induction of Clinical Hypnosis and Forms of Indirect Suggestion.* New York: Irvington.
A classic from the godfather of hypnotherapy.

Haley, J. (1993). *Uncommon Therapy: The Psychiatric Techniques of Milton H.
Erickson, M.D.* New York: W. W. Norton & Company.
A look at Erickson through communication theory and strategic therapy lenses.

Gilligan, S. G. (1987). *Therapeutic Trances: The Cooperation Principle in Ericksonian Hypnotherapy.* New York: Brunner/Mazel.
*By one of the best teachers around who also runs the famous Trance Camp, a good
place to learn how to do the work.*

Hammond, D. C. (Ed.). (1990). *Handbook of Hypnotic Suggestions and Metaphors.*
New York: W. W. Norton & Company .

Bandler, R., & Grinder, J. (1975). *The Structure of Magic: A Book About Language
and Therapy,* and *The Structure of Magic II: A Book About Communication and
Change.* Palo Alto, CA: Science and Behavior Books.
*Bandler and Grinder filmed the best therapists of the early 1970s and deconstructed
exactly what the therapists did, systemized what they found, and wrote books about
it. Milton Erickson was their most discussed subject. These are valuable books for
any therapist.*

Somatic Therapies

Stanley, S. (2016). *Relational and Body-Centered Practices for Healing Trauma.*
New York: Routledge.

Arielle Schwartz and Barb Maiberger's *EMDR Therapy and Somatic Psychology*

(2018) *A lovely, deep, and user-friendly book about the merging of the two therapies. They show how fluidly the somatic therapies can merge with any other therapy.*

For assessing your client's place in their culture

Brown, L. (2008). *Cultural Competence in Trauma Therapy: Beyond the Flashback.* Washington, DC: American Psychological Association.

References

Alcoholics Anonymous. (2019). *What is A.A.?* Retrieved from https://www.aa
.org/pages/en_US/what-is-aa

American Psychiatric Association. (2013). *Diagnostic and statistical manual of
mental disorders* (5th ed.). Washington, DC: American Psychiatric Association.

Ainsworth, M. D. S., Blehar, M. C., Waters, E., & Wall, S. (1978). *Patterns of
attachment: A psychological study of the strange situation.* Hillsday, NJ: Lawrence
Erlbaum.

Arad, H. (2018). *Integrating Relational Psychoanalysis and EMDR.* New York:
Routledge.

Aron, E. (1996). *The Highly Sensitive Person.* New York: Citadel Press.

Baek, J., Lee, S., Cho, T., Kim, S.-W., Kim, M., Yoon, Y., & Shin, H.-S. (2019).
Neural circuits underlying a psychotherapeutic regimen for fear disorders.
Nature, 566(7744), 339–343. doi.org/10.1038/s41586-019-0931-y

Bandler, R., & Grinder, J. (1975). *The Structure of Magic: A Book About Language
and Therapy.* Palo Alto, CA: Science and Behavior Books.

Bandler, R., & Grinder, J. (1975). *The Structure of Magic II: A Book About Communication and Change.* Palo Alto, CA: Science and Behavior Books.

Beck, J. (2011). *Cognitive Behavior Therapy: Basics and Beyond* (2nd ed.). New
York: Guilford Press.

Beck, A., Rush, J., Shaw, B., & Emery, G. (1987). *Cognitive Therapy of Depression.*
New York: Guilford Press.

Beck, A. T., Ward, C. H., Mendelson, M., Mock, J., & Erbaugh, J. (1961). An
inventory for measuring depression. *Archives of General Psychiatry, 4,* 561–571.

Bernstein, E. M., & Putnam, F. W. (1986). Development, reliability, and validity of a dissociation scale. *Journal of Nervous & Mental Disease, 174,* 727–735.

Boon, S., Steele, K., & van der Hart, O. (2011) *Coping with Trauma-Related Dissociation, Skills Training for Patients and Therapists.* New York: W. W. Norton & Company.

Bowlby, J. (1988). *A Secure Base: Parent-child attachment and healthy human development.* New York: Basic Books.

Brown, L. (2008). *Cultural competence in trauma therapy: Beyond the flashback.* Washington, DC: American Psychological Association.

Burns, D. (1992). *Feeling Good, The New Mood Therapy.* New York: Morrow/Avon Press.

Burns, D. (1992). *The Feeling Good Handbook.* New York: Penguin.

Calof, D. (1996). *The Couple Who Became Each Other and Other Tales of Healing from a Hypnotherapist's Casebook.* New York: Bantam

Centers for Disease Control and Prevention. (2016). *Suicide rates rose across the US from 1999 to 2016.* Retrieved from https://www.cdc.gov/media/releases/2018/p0607-suicide-prevention.html

Cuddy, A. (2012). *Your body language may shape who you are.* Retrieved from https://www.ted.com/talks/amy_cuddy_your_body_language_shapes _who_you_are?language=en

Damasio, A. (1999). *The feeling of what happens: body and emotion in the making of consciousness* (pp. 133–167). New York: Harcourt.

Davanloo, H. (2000). *Intensive Short-Term Dynamic Psychotherapy: Selected papers of Habib Davanloo, MD.* New York: Wiley.

de Becker, G. (1997). *The Gift of Fear and Other Survival Signals that Protect Us from Violence.* New York: Random House, Inc.

Erickson, M., Rossi, E., & Rossi, S. (1976). *Hypnotic Realities: The Induction of Clinical Hypnosis and Forms of Indirect Suggestion.* New York: Irvington.

Felitti, V., Anda, R., Nordenberg, D., Williamson, D., Spitz, A., Edwards, V., . . . Marks, J. (1998). Relationship of Childhood Abuse and Household Dysfunction to Many of the Leading Causes of Death in Adults. *American Journal of Preventive Medicine. 14*(4), 245–258.

Foa, E. B., Hembree, E. A., & Rothbaum, B. O. (2007). *Prolonged exposure therapy for PTSD: Emotional processing of traumatic experiences, therapist guide.* New York: Oxford University Press.

Forgash, C., & Copeley, M. (2008). *Healing the Heart of Trauma and Dissociation with EMDR and ego state therapy.* New York: Springer.

Fosha, D. (2000). *The Transforming Power of Affect: A model for accelerated change.* New York: Basic Books.

Frank, J. D. (1961). *Persuasion and Healing: a comparative study of psychotherapy.* Baltimore, MD: Johns Hopkins Press.

Gilligan, S. (1987). *Therapeutic Trances: The Cooperation Principle in Ericksonian Hypnotherapy.* New York: Brunner/Mazel.

Greenberger, D., & Padesky, C. A. (2016). *Mind Over Mood: Change How You Feel by Changing the Way You Think* (2nd ed.). New York: Guilford Press.

Hammond, D. C. (Ed.). (1990). *Handbook of Hypnotic Suggestions and Metaphors.* New York: W. W. Norton & Company.

Kelly, J. F., & Yeterian, J. D. (2008). Mutual-help groups. In W. O'Donohue & J. R. Cunningham (Eds.), *Evidence-Based Adjunctive Treatments* (pp. 61–105). New York: Elsevier.

Kitchur, M. (2005). The strategic developmental model for EMDR. In R. Shapiro (Ed.), *EMDR solutions: Pathways to Healing* (pp. 8–56). New York: W. W. Norton & Company.

Knipe, J. (2005). Targeting Positive Affect to Clear the Pain of Unrequited Love, Codependence, Avoidance, and Procrastination. In R. Shapiro (Ed.), *EMDR solutions: Pathways to Healing* (pp. 189–212). New York: W. W. Norton & Company.

Knipe, J. (2008). "Shame is My Safe Place." In R. Shapiro (Ed.), *EMDR Solutions II, for Depression, Eating Disorders, Performance, and More.* New York: W. W. Norton & Company.

Kubler-Ross, E. (2005). *On Grief and Grieving: Finding the Meaning of Grief Through the Five Stages of Loss.* New York: Simon & Schuster.

Jaborandi, N., Greenwald, R., Rubin, A., Oliaee, S. O., & Shiva, Z. (2004). A comparison of CBT and EMDR for sexually-abused Iranian girls. *Clinical Psychology and Psychotherapy.* Retrieved from https://onlinelibrary.wiley.com/doi/abs/10.1002/cpp.395

Levine, P. (1997). *Waking the tiger: Healing trauma.* Berkeley: North Atlantic Books.

Linehan, M. (1993). *Skills Training Manual for Treating Borderline Personality Disorder.* New York: Guildford Press.

Luxenberg, T., Spinazzola, J., & van der Kolk, B. A. (2001). Complex traumas and disorders of extreme stress (DESNOS) diagnoses, Part I: Assessment. *Directions in Psychiatry, 21,* lesson 25. Retrieved from http://www.traumacenter.org/products/pdf_files/DESNOS.pdf

Maiberger, B. (2009). *EMDR Essentials: a guide for clients and therapists.* New York: W. W. Norton & Company.

Main, M. (1991). Metacognitive knowledge, metacognitive monitoring and singular (coherent) versus multiple (incoherent) models of attachment: Findings and directions for further research. In C. Parkes, J. Stevenson-Hinde, & P. Marris (Eds.), *Attachment across the life cycle* (pp. 127–159). London: Routledge.

Masterson, J. F. (1981). *The Narcissistic and Borderline Disorders.* New York: Brunner Mazel.

McGoldrick, M., Gerson, R., S., & Petri, S. S. (2008). *Genograms: Assessment and Intervention.* (3rd ed.) New York: W. W. Norton & Company.

Miller, P. W. (2016). *EMDR Therapy for Schizophrenia and Other Psychoses.* New York: Springer Publishing Company.

Miller, R. (2012). Treatment of behavioral addictions utilizing the feeling-state addiction protocol: A multiple baseline study. *Journal of EMDR Practice and Research, 6(4),* 159–169.

Miller, W. R., Zweben, A., DiClemente, C. C., & Rychtarik, R. G. (1992). *Motivational Enhancement Therapy Manual.* Washington, DC: National Institute on Alcohol Abuse and Alcoholism.

National Institute of Mental Health. (2019). *Suicide.* Retrieved from https://www.nimh.nih.gov/health/statistics/suicide.shtml

Ogden P., Minton, K., & Pain, C. (2006). *Trauma and the body: A sensorimotor approach to psychotherapy.* New York: W. W. Norton & Company.

Pace, P. (2007). *Lifespan Integration: Connecting ego-states through time.* Retrieved from www.lifespanintegration.com

Paulsen, S. (2009). *Looking through the Eyes of Trauma and Dissociation.* South Carolina: Booksurge Publishing.

Popky, A. (2005). DeTur, an Urge Reduction Protocol for Addictions and Dysfunctional Behaviors. In R. Shapiro (Ed.), *EMDR Solutions: Pathways to Healing.* New York: W. W. Norton & Company.

Porges, S. (2017). *The Pocket guide to The Polyvagal Theory.* New York: W. W. Norton & Company.

Rosen, D. H. (1975). Suicide survivors—A follow-up study of persons who survived jumping from the Golden Gate and San Francisco-Oakland Bay Bridges. *Western Journal of Medicine.* Apr;122(4):289-94.

Rosenberg, M. (2012). *Living Nonviolent Communication: practical tools to connect and communicate skillfully in every situation.* Boulder, CO: Sounds True, Inc.

Schnarch, D. (1991). *Constructing the Sexual Crucible.* New York: W. W. Norton & Company.

Schore, A. N. (1994). *Affect regulation and the origin of the self: The neurobiology of emotional development.* Hillsdale, NJ: Erlbaum.

Schwartz. A., & Maiberger, B. (2018). *EMDR Therapy and Somatic Psychology.* New York: W. W. Norton & Company.

Segal, Z., Williams, M., & Teasdale, J. (2013). *Mindfulness-based cognitive therapy for depression.* New York: Guilford Press.

Segal, Z., Williams, M., & Teasdale, J. (2014). *The Mindful Way Workbook.* New York: Guilford Press.

Seligman, M. E. P. (1991). *Helplessness: On Depression, Development, and Death.* Second edition. New York: W. H. Freeman

Servan-Schreiber, D. (2004). *The Instinct to Heal.* New York: Rodale Press.

Servan-Schreiber, D., Schooler, J., Dew, M. A., Carter, C., & Bartone, P. (2006). Eye Movement Desensitization and Reprocessing for Posttraumatic Stress Disorder: A Pilot Blinded, Randomized Study of Stimulation Type. *Psychotherapy and Psychosomatics, 75,* 290–297. doi: 10.1159/000093950

Shapiro, F. (2001). *Eye Movement Desensitization and Reprocessing.* New York: Guilford Press.

Shapiro, F. (2012). *Getting Past your Past: Take control of your life with self-help techniques from EMDR therapy.* New York: Rodale.

Shapiro, F. (2017). *Eye Movement Desensitization and Reprocessing.* New York: Guilford Press.

Shapiro, R. (2005a). EMDR with Cultural and Generational Introjects. In Shapiro (Ed.) *EMDR Solutions: Pathways to Healing.* New York: W. W. Norton & Company.

Shapiro, R. (2005b). The Two-Hand Interweave. In Shapiro (Ed.) *EMDR Solutions: Pathways to Healing.* New York: W. W. Norton & Company

Shapiro, R. (2008). *EMDR Solutions II, For Depression, Eating Disorders, Performance, and More.* New York: W. W. Norton & Company.

Shapiro, R. (2010). *The Trauma Treatment Handbook, Protocols Across the Spectrum.* New York: W. W. Norton & Company.

Shapiro, R. (2018). *Visual Aids for Psychotherapy.* Seattle: Self-published.

Shapiro, R. (2016). *Easy Ego State Interventions.* New York: W. W. Norton & Company.

Sheldon, B. W., & Sheldon, A. (in press). *Complex Integration of Multiple Brain*

Systems in Therapy; Building Failsafe Neural Networks. New York: W. W. Norton & Company.

Siegel, D. J. (1999). *The developing mind: Toward a neurobiology of interpersonal experience*. New York: Guilford Press.

Sprowls, C., & Marquis, P. (2013, September). The neurobiology and treatment of obsessive compulsive disorders utilizing EMDR. Presentation at the 18th EMDR International Association Conference, Austin, TX.

Stanley, S. (2016). *Relational and Body-Centered Practices for Healing Trauma*. New York: Routledge.

Steele, A. (2007a). *I'm So Glad You're Here* [CD]. Available at http://april-steele.ca/apr/imaginal-nurturing-cds/

Steele, A. (2007b). *Developing a Secure Self Book and Therapeutic Toolkit*. Retrieved from http://april-steele.ca/apr/developing-secure-self-handbook-therapeutic-toolkit/

Steele, K., Boon, S., & van der Hart, O. (2017). *Treating Trauma-Related Dissociation*. New York: W. W. Norton & Company.

Taibbi, R. (2016). *The Art of the First Session*. New York: W. W. Norton & Company.

Tronick, E. (2009). *Still Face Experiment: Dr. Edward Tronick* [video] UMass Boston. ZERO TO THREE. https://www.youtube.com/watch?v=apzXGEbZht0

van der Hart, O., Nijenhuis, E., & Steele, K. (2006). *The haunted self: Structural dissociation and the treatment of chronic traumatization*. New York: W. W. Norton & Company.

van der Kolk, B. A., Spinazzola, J., Blaustein, M. E., Hopper, J. W., Hopper, E. K., Korn, D. L., & Simpson, W. B. (2007). A randomized clinical trial of eye movement desensitization and reprocessing (EMDR), fluoxetine, and pill placebo in the treatment of posttraumatic stress disorder: treatment effects and long-term maintenance. *Journal of Clinical Psychiatry, 68*(1), 37–46.

Watkins, H. & Watkins, J. (1997). *Ego States: Theory and Therapy*. New York: W. W. Norton & Company.

Wolpe, J. (1958). *Psychotherapy by reciprocal inhibition*. Stanford, CA: Stanford University Press.

Wong, J., & Brown, J. (2017, June 6). How Gratitude Changes You and Your Brain. *Greater Good Magazine*. Retrieved from https://greatergood.berkeley.edu/article/item/how_gratitude_changes_you_and_your_brain

Index

Note: Italicized page locators refer to figures.

bodywork, 104
borderline personality disorder (BPD), 54, 111
  anxious-ambivalent attachment and, 93
  attachment issues and, 98–99, 100
  chronic suicidal ideation and, 131
  emotional parts of people with, 119
boundaries, 101, 206
  basic, 67–69
  for protection of both client and therapist, 76
  repairing dysfunctional attachment and, 95
Bowlby, J., 94
BPD. *see* borderline personality disorder (BPD)
breathing exercises, 205
Brown, J., 109
bullying, 79
  clearing past traumas of, 80
  suicidal ideation and, 140
  suicide risk and, 129
burnout
  knowing signs of, 205
  trauma clients and, 204

Cabassi, S., 23
caffeine, anxiety and, 148
calm-down techniques, 74, 195
cancellations
  Client Information Form, 42
  notices of, 41
CBT. *see* cognitive behavioral therapy (CBT)
Center for Nonviolent Communication, 110

Centers for Disease Control and Prevention, 128
chemical imbalance, chronic depression and, 190
child abuse, 204
  complex traumatic stress disorders and, 114
  dissociative responses to, 85
  shame-based depression and, 191–92
choices, making, 104–5
chronic depression, causes of, 178, 190–91
chronic fatigue syndrome, depressive symptoms and, 182
chronic suicidal ideation
  client assessment and, 131–32
  ritually-abused DID clients with, 139–40
CIMBS. *see* Complex Integration of Multiple Brain Systems (CIMBS)
claustrophobia, 147
Client Information Form, 42–45
  appointments, 42
  cancellations, 42
  complaints and unprofessional conduct, 45
  confidentiality, 43–44
  confidentiality and insurance, 44
  contact information, 42
  declining my services, 44–45
  fees, 42
  insurance billing, 42
  online communication, 44
  privacy practices, 42–43
clients
  assessing for suicide risk, 130–31
  long-term, saying goodbye to, 202

trauma-informed model of genograms, 49

trauma therapy
  for addiction, 168
  for depression, 179–80

Treating Trauma-Related Dissociation (Steele, Boon, & van der Hart), 126

treatment plans, 60–62
  client goals and course of treatment, 61–62
  for clients with multiple diagnoses, 60
  components of, 60

triggers
  bingeing, 171
  for panic attacks, 156
  for suicidal ideation, 130

"Triple Warmer" meridian, calming, 36

Tronick, E., 86

twelve-step programs, 165–67, 170

Two-Hand technique, 79, 81, 105
  for anxious clients, 150
  for differentiating current sexual partner from abuser, 196–97
  performance anxiety and, 157

unmyelinated ventral vagus
  depression and, 177
  PTSD and, 178
  trauma and, 113

Vagal Hold
  for anxious clients, 149
  panic attacks and, 155

vagus nerve, 177
  calming, 36
  trauma and, 113

van der Hart, O., 118

van der Kolk, B., 179, 187

ventral vagus, 113, 177, 178

vicarious trauma, 204, 205

violence, clearing past traumas of, 80

virtual reality, 123

vitamin D, depression treatment and, 189

white privilege, 78

window of tolerance, 56

withdrawal, from drugs and alcohol, 164

women suicide attempts by, 129

Wong, J., 109

World Health Organization, 183

yoga, 189, 205, 206

younger parts of self, clients with phobia of, 99–100

Ziatz, S., 23

Zweben, A., 161